OTAKAR ŠEVČÍK Op. 17

Wieniawski Violin Concerto in D minor
Complete Piano & Violin Score
Critical Urtext Violin Part

Analytical Studies & Exercises

Edited by Endre Granat

Introduction

By Endre Granat

Henryk Wieniawski was one of the most brilliant violinists of the post-Paganini generation. He was born in Lublin (Poland) in 1835 and began musical studies at the age of 5 under the tutelage of his mother, an excellent pianist. In 1843, Wieniawski was admitted into the Paris Conservatoire and soon joined the class of Lambert Massart, the famed disciple of Kreutzer. He continued his studies at the Conservatoire until 1850, when he received the Premier Prix, both as violinist and composer at the precocious age of 15.

Wieniawski's concert career began while still a student at the Conservatoire. He performed with unprecedented success throughout Europe, the Mideast, Northern Africa and America. From 1860-1872, Wieniawski served as the Soloist to the Czar and Professor at the newly established St.Petersburg Conservatory. In 1875, he became the head of the violin department of the Brussels Conservatoire. Among his students was Eugène Ysaÿe.

Wieniawski's style of playing was vastly different from any of the virtuosos of the violin who preceded him. He combined the classical approach of violin technique that he learned from Massart with the expression of his passionate musical personality. He was the first string player who used an expressive vibrato. His tone production was far superior to his contemporaries. His playing style, approach to violin playing and innovative bowing became the template of the famed Russian Violin School. Wieniawski's bow hold became known as the " Russian bow grip ".

Wieniawski died in Moscow in 1880, at only 45 years old.

Wieniawski's legacy as a composer is substantial. There are twenty-four works with opus numbers, nine without opus numbers in print and some thirty works still in manuscript. His best-known works are his Scherzo-Tarantelle, the two Polonaises and the two Violin Concertos. Although not as well known to audiences, his Ecole Moderne and Etudes-Caprices are standard staples in every conservatory.

The Violin Concerto in d minor op.22 shows Wieniawski the composer in his full maturity. The thematic material ranges from the beautifully lyrical first movement to the fiery a la Zingara. The virtuoso violin part is brilliantly written.

The composer first presented this concerto in 1862 in St.Petersburg. Even though the performance was a rousing success, Wieniawski rewrote and condensed the piece during the next six years. In 1868 he performed the work in its present form. The concerto is dedicated to Pablo de Sarasate.

This edition is based on the original orchestra score and the original violin piano reduction, both printed in 1870 by Schott in Mainz, Germany. Tempo indications and nuances by the editor are in parenthesis.

I would like to express my sincere gratitude to Katarzyna Kulagowska-Urbaniak, Musical Collection Specialist at the Henryk Wieniawski Musical Society in Poznan, Poland, for providing source material and contributing her wisdom to this project.

VORWORT ZU DEN KONZERTSTUDIEN OPUS 17—21.

Um die Möglichkeit einer absoluten Sicherheit für die Reproduktion eines Werkes zu schaffen, ist es notwendig, daß man sich den einzelnen Teilen auf analytischem Wege nähert. Nur so erzielt man technische, dynamische u. s. w. Wirkungen. Der Individualität des Spielers, dessen musikalische Urteilskraft auf diesem Wege ausgebildet und geschärft wird, sollen hierdurch die Richtlinien für eine eigene, durch die intuitiven Komponenten der Seele bestimmte Entwicklung gegeben werden. Die Analogie erschließt dann weite Welten, neuer ungeahnten Möglichkeiten. Nach dem Durchstudieren der einzelnen Intervall- und analytischen Studien — bei ständiger Beachtung der dynamischen Vortragszeichen — schreite man sofort an die entsprechende Taktgruppe der Solostimme heran, auf diese Weise erwächst ein von technischen Schwierigkeiten befreiter, beseelter und schlechthin vollkommener, idealer Violinvortrag. Aus dem langsamen Tempo soll sich mit Rücksicht auf eine eventuelle Orchesterbegleitung ein möglichst rhytmisierter Vortragsstil entwickeln. Insofern weitere Voraussetzungen und Regeln, die auf das Violinspiel vom technischen und interpretierenden Standpunkt Bezug haben, in Betracht kommen, verweise ich auf das Vorwort und den analytischen Teil in meinem Opus 16. Guter Wille, Ausdauer und Fleiß sind die Seele dieses Werkes. Möge die Gewissenhaftigkeit der Analyse den Spieler nicht abschrecken, vielmehr soll sie in ihm die Liebe zur Lösung weiterer Probleme erwecken, umso besser erkennt er dann das Wesen des Musikalisch-Schönen in all seinen subtilsten Bestandteilen. Inwieweit mir dies gelungen ist, soll der Erfolg des Studiums entscheiden. Einzelne Steine aus dem großen, prachtvollen Mosaik der Meisterwerke, die mit Fleiß geschliffen werden, mögen im hellen, sonnigen Glanz der vom Gefühl belebten Seele erstrahlen. Es sei hier auch meinem Assistenten Herrn V. Nopp für die hervorragende und hilfsbereite Unterstützung bei den schwierigen Korrekturen der Vortragsschule und der Konzertstudien und dem Herrn Verleger für die sorgfältige Herausgabe meines Werkes der Dank ausgesprochen. Und wenn jemand mit jenem Fleiß, jener Überlegung und veredelnder Liebe, von denen ich mich bei der Schaffung des Werkes leiten ließ, an das Opus herantritt, dann werde ich zur Genüge belohnt sein.

Písek, im Sommer 1929 *Prof. Ot. Ševčík*

PREFACE TO THE CONCERT STUDIES OP. 17—21.

An analytic study of the separate parts of a work is essential to guarantee a safe reproduction of the whole. Only by these means technical, dynamic and other effects are to be gained. Thus a criterion shall be given to the individuality of the player, whose musical judgement is developed and sharpened in this way, for a development of its own, determined by the intuitive components of the soul. Great worlds of new unthought-of possibilities will then be disclosed by analogy. After having studied the separate interval and analytic studies, always observing the dynamic signs of execution, one may immediately turn to the respective group of bars of the solo voice; thus an inspired, absolute perfect and ideal execution, rid from technical difficulties, is obtained. With regard to an eventual accompaniment by orchestra a style of execution as rhythmical as possible shall develop out of the slow time. As far as further preliminaries and rules referring to the violin playing from a technical and interpreting standpoint may be concerned, I refer to the preface and analytic part of my op. 16. Good will, perseverance and zeal are the soul of the work. The scrupulousness of the analysis shall not frighten the player, but rather awaken in him a desire for solving further problems, thus enabling him to distinguish the better the nature of the musically beautiful in its subtlest components. The success of the studies shall decide how far I have succeeded herein. Detached stones out of the great magnificent mosaic of the masterpieces, cut with diligence, may resplend in the bright sunny radiance of the inspired soul. At the same time I want to thank my assistent Mr. V. Nopp for his valuable and ever-ready help in regard to the wearisome proofs of the School of interpretation and the Concert Studies and the publisher for his careful edition of my work. If some players approach this opus with the same zeal, deliberation and ennobling love as I have been guided by at the making of the work, I shall be sufficiently rewarded.

Písek, Summer 1929 *Prof. Ot. Ševčík*

AVANT-PROPOS AUX „ETUDES DE CONCERT" OP. 17—21.

Pour atteindre, dans la limite du possible, la sûreté absolue concernant l'exécution d'un ouvrage, il faut procéder à l'analyse des diverses parties de cette oeuvre. Ce n'est qu'à cette condition qu'on atteint aux effets techniques, dynamiques, etc. Par cela même, les directives d'un développement spécial et caractérisé par les affinités de l'âme doivent être imprimées à l'individualité de l'exécutant qui perfectionne et aiguise son jugement de cette manière. De plus, l'analyse ouvre des mondes vastes, des possibilités jamais pressenties avant cet examen. Après avoir étudié les différents exercices d'intervalles et d'analyse, en observant scrupuleusement les indications détaillées, on apprend le groupe de mesures qui est conforme à la partie de violon. De cette manière, il en résulte une exécution instrumentale animée, tendant à la perfection et libre de difficultés. Le mouvement lent demande, autant que possible, un style d'exécution large et rhythmique en accord avec l'accompagnement d'orchestre. En considération des règles et des suggestions concernant l'exécution technique et l'interprétation, je vous indique l'avant-propos et la partie analytique de mon op. 16. La bonne volonté, l'assiduité et la persévérance sont la base de cet ouvrage. Que la délicatesse de conscience de l'analyse ne décourage pas l'exécutant; mais, au contraire, qu'elle éveille en son âme le désir de résoudre encore d'autres problèmes qu'il solutionnera de mieux en mieux, puis il découvrira l'âme du beau en musique dans tous ses éléments les plus subtils. De la façon de travailler dépend le succès. Que les différentes pierres de la mosaïque superbe, enchâssées avec art rayonnent et scintillent de leurs feux dans la clarté brillante, comme le soleil de l'âme animée par le sentiment! Je tiens à remercier spécialement Monsieur mon assistant V. Nopp de son aide efficace et aimable des corrections pénibles de l'école d'interprétation et des Etudes de concert et de plus Monsieur l'éditeur de cet ouvrage du soin tout particulier qu'il a apporté à cette collaboration. Je veux également ajouter que si la création de ces études peut inciter quelque travailleur à s'adonner à cet ouvrage avec diligence et réflexion, je me sentirai bien largement récompensé.

Písek, été 1929 *Prof. Ot. Ševčík*

PREÁMBULO Á LOS ESTUDIOS DE CONCIERTO OP. 17—21.

Para alcanzar, en los limites de lo posible, la seguridad absoluta en la ejecución de una obra es preciso efectuar el análisis de sus diversas partes. Solo con esta condición se consiguen los efectos técnicos, dinámicos, etc. Por este mismo medio, las directivas de un desarrollo especial y caracterizado por las afinidades del alma deben imprimirse en la individualidad del ejecutante, quien, de esta manera, perfecciona y afina su interpretación. Además el análisis descubre amplios horizontes, posibilidades nunca presentidas antes de este examen. Después de haber estudiado los diferentes ejercicios de intérvalos y el análisis teniendo en cuenta escrupulosamente las indicaciones detalladas, debe de aprenderse el grupo de compases que se refiere a la parte de violín. De esta manera, se consigue una ejecución instrumental animada, con miras a la perfección y exenta de dificultades. El movimiento lento requiere, dentro de lo posible, un estilo de ejecución amplio y rítmico en relación con el acompañamiento de la orquesta. Por lo que se refiere á las reglas y sugestiones relacionadas con la ejecución técnica y la interpretación, me remito al preámbulo y parte analítica de mi op. 16. La buena voluntad, asiduidad y perseverancia son los necesarios fundamentos de este trabajo. La delicadeza de conciencia en el análisis no debe desanimar al ejecutante, antes bien ha de despertar en su alma el deseo de resolver también otros problemas cuya resolución le resultará más y más perfecta, hasta llegar á descubrir la esencia de lo bello en música, incluso en sus matices más exquisitos. De la manera de trabajar depende el éxito. Como las diferentes piedras de un soberbio mosaico, armonicamente engarzadas, brillan e irradian sus fuegos en una espléndida claridad, así resplandece el sol del alma, animada por el sentimiento. Sean expresadas mis sinceras gracias a mi asistente V. Nopp por su amable ayuda en las trabajosas correcciones de la Escuela de Ejecución de Violín y Estudios de Concierto y no menos al editor de mi obra por los exquisitos cuidados que a ella ha dedicado. Y asimismo si la creación de estos estudios estimulara algun voluntarioso á dedicarse con diligencia y reflexión á esta clase de trabajo tendría en ello la mejor de las recompensas.

Písek, verano de 1929 *Prof. Ot. Ševčík*

ÚVOD KE STUDIU KONCERTNÍMU OP. 17—21.

Aby byla dána možnost naprosté jistoty reprodukce díla, jest nutno k jednotlivým jeho částem se blížiti cestou analytickou. Jen tak lze dosáhnouti bezprostřední působivosti technické, dynamické atd. Individualitě hráčově, jehož hudební úsudek touto cestou byl vycvičen a zostřen, mají býti dány směrnice pro vlastní její vývoj, daný intuitivními složkami duše. Analogie nechť pak otevírá široké obzory nekonečných možností dalších. Po prostudování jednotlivých studií intervalových a analytických, se stálým zřetelem k dynamickým znaménkům, budiž přistoupeno ihned k téže skupině taktové v hlase sólovém; tímto způsobem z neomylně ovládaných požadavků technických, stavších se mimoděk prvkem podružným, vzejde ideál houslové hry oduševnělé a hodnotně dokonalé. Z tempa volného nechť vzrůstá styl přednesu co nejrytmičtějšího se zřetelem k případnému provedení s doprovodem orchestrálním. Pokud nutno dbáti všech předpokladů ostatních i pravidel, týkajících se hry houslové s hlediska technického i přednesového, poukazuji na obsahovou stránku úvodu a analytické části ve svém opusu č. 16. Dobrá vůle, trpělivost a snaha jsou duší tohoto díla. Svědomitost rozboru nechť nezalekne hráče, naopak, kéž probudí v něm lásku k řešení problémů dalších, o to lépe pozná podstatu hudebního krásna ve všech jeho nejsubtilnějších součástkách. V jaké míře se mi to podařilo, budiž ponecháno k rozhodnutí výsledkům studia. Jednotlivé kameny velké, nádherné mosaiky díla mistrů, pílí vybroušené, nechť zazáří jasným slunným světlem duše žijící citem. Budiž vyjádřen dík mému asistentu p. V. Noppovi za vydatnou a ochotnou pomoc při namáhavých korekturách Školy přednesu a Studií a p. nakladateli za vkusnou úpravu mého díla. Přistoupí-li kdo k dílu s onou pílí, rozvahou a zušlechťující láskou, s níž jsem přistoupil k němu já, budu dostatečně odměněn.

V Písku v létě 1929 *Prof. Ot. Ševčík*

WSTĘP DO STUDJUM KONCERTOWEGO OP. 17—21.

Chcąc osiągnąć pewność doskonałą w reprodukcji danego dzieła, musimy rozpocząć studyrowanie analizującym sposobem, każdej części z osobna. Tylko w ten sposób możemy osiągnąć bezpośredni wynik w technice, dynamice i t. d. Indywidualności grającego, którego krytycyzm muzyczny tą drogą został udoskonalony, musi być dany pewien kierunek dla wewnętrznego rozwoju, kierunek, nadany intuicją duchową. Niech potem analogja otwiera szerokie horyzonty najdalej idących możliwości. Po wyćwiczeniu każdego interwału z osobna, jak i po studjum analizacyjnem, zwracając przy tem stale uwagę na znaki dynamiczne, przystępujemy zaraz do ćwiczenia tejże grupy taktów części solowej; tym sposobem, z tych bez zarzutu opanowanych technicznych trudności, jakie mimowolnie były elementami podrzędnemi, powstanie ideał uduchowionej i doskonałej gry na skrzypcach. Przy wolnem tempie powinien wystąpić styl jak najbardziej rytmicznej gry, ze względu na ewentualny akompaniament orkiestralny. Wszystkie uwagi, odnoszące się do reguły, która ma za treść techniczną i interpretacyj ną stronę gry na skrzypcach, zamieszczam we wstępnem słowie i analizacyjnej części mego Opusu No. 16. Duszą wykonanego dzieła są: dobra wola, cierpliwość i staranność. Sumienność, jaką wymaga analiza, nie powinna odstraszać grającego — przeciwnie, powinna w nim wzbudzić ochotę do dalszego rozwiązywania nowych zagadnień; dopiero wtedy pozna grający istotę piękna w muzyce, nawet w jej najsubtelniejszych cząstkach. W jakim stopniu udało mi się to osiągnąć, niech wynik studja rozstrzygnie. Pojedyncze kamienie olbrzymiej, przepięknej mozaiki wielu mistrzów, jakie pilnie szlifowane były, niech rozświecą jasnem światłem słonecznem duszy, uczuciami żyjącej. Panu Wydawcy składam podziękowanie za staranne wydanie mego dzieła; a gdy ktokolwiek do tego dzieła przystąpi z tą pilnością, rozwagą i uszlachetniającą miłością, jak ja to uczyniłem, — będę dostatecznie wynagrodzony.

Písek w lecie 1929 *Prof. Ot. Ševčík*

INTRODUZIONE ALLO STUDIO ANALITICO DEI CONCERTI, OPUS 17—21.

Per eseguire un'opera con sicurezza assoluta bisogna avvicinarsi alle sue singole parti in modo analitico. Soltanto così si può raggiungere una immediata efficacia tecnica, dinamica ecc. All'individualità del sonatore il cui giudizio musicale è stato in questo modo perfezionato ed acuminato si debbono dare le norme per il suo sviluppo proprio determinato dalle parti intuitive dell'anima. L'analogia apra poi i vasti orizzonti delle infinite altre possibilità. — Dopo aver studiati i singoli esercizi analitici degl' intervalli, tenendo sempre conto di segni dinamici, il violinista si metta subito a studiare il rispettivo gruppo di misure nella parte del solo; in questo modo dai postulati tecnici, compiuti alla perfezione e diventati istintivamente elemento secondario, sorge l'ideale del modo perfetto ed ingentilito di sonare il violino. Del tempo lento si sviluppi lo stile dell' esposizione più ritmica quanto si voglia, col riguardo alla eventuale esecuzione coll' accompagnamento dell' orchestra. Per quanto si riferisce a tutte le altre supposizioni ed alle regole concernenti il modo di sonare il violino in riguardo di tecnica e di esposizione richiamo l'attenzione dei violinisti all' introduzione ed alle parti analitiche del mio Opus No 16. Buona volontà, pazienza e zelo sono l'anima dell' opera presente. La coscienziosità nell' analisi non scoraggi il sonatore ma, al contrario, risvegli in lui l'amore a risolvere i problemi più difficili affinchè meglio conosca la sostanza del bello musicale in tutti i suoi particolari più sottili. A qual termine io sia riuscito a raggiungere questo scopo ne decidano gli effetti dello studio fatto a base di quest'opera. Le singole pietre del grande, magnifico mosaico dell'opera dei maestri, forbite per diligenza, brillino con chiara soleggiata luce dell'anima vivente nel sentimento. Ringrazio vivamente il mio assistente Sig. V. Nopp del suo abbondante e gentile aiuto nel faticoso correggere le bozze della Scuola dell' esposizione e dello Studio, e il Sig. editore per aver provveduto all' esteriore della mia opera con molto gusto, e sarò ricompensato abbastanza se i violinisti si metteranno a studiarla con tale diligenza, considerazione e nobilitante amore con la quale io mi sono accinto a scriverla.

Písek, d'estate 1929 *Prof. Ottacaro Ševčík*

ПРЕДИСЛОВИЕ К КОНЦЕРТНЫМ УПРАЖНЕНИЯМ ОР. 17—21.

Чтобы дать возможность абсолютно правильного исполнения музыкального произведения, необходимо к его отдельным частям подойти с анализом. Лишь таким образом можно достигнуть прямого воздействия техники, динамики и т. д. Личности исполнителя, который таким путем приобрел и углубил свое суждение, необходимы направляющие начала его развития, данные интуицией его души. Путь аналогии откроет широкие горизонты неограниченных дальнейших возможностей. По окончании отдельных интервaловых и аналитических упражнений, обращая при этом внимание на динамические знаки, приступим тотчас же в тех же отрывках к партии сольной. Таким образом, овладев вполне техническими требованиями, которые сами собой станут элементом второстепенным, достигнем идеала скрипичной игры — игры одухотворенной и совершенной. Медленные темпы могут нам дать исполнение ритмически точное, что необходимо при исполнении с аккомпаниментом оркестра. Что же касается всех остальных условий и правил скрипичной игры со стороны технической и исполнения, то обращаю внимание на введение и аналитическую часть своего оп. № 16. Охота, терпение и стремление — главное в этих занятиях. Пусть подробный разбор не пугает исполнителя, а наоборот — пробудит в нем интерес к решению дальнейших проблем и тем самым приведет его к пониманию красоты музыки, во всех ее тончайших проявлениях. Хороший результат ваших занятий будет наилучшим судьей моего труда. Пусть отдельные самоцветные камни большой и дивной мозаики произведений музыкальных мастеров, отшлифованные искусством исполнения, засияют ясным солнечным светом души чувствующей. Выражаю благодарность моему ассистенту г. В. Ноппу за существенную и любезную помощь при тяжелых исправлениях »Школы скрипичной игры« и настоящих »Концертных этюдов«. Г. издателя благодарю за изящное издание моего труда. Если всякий подойдет к нему с тем усердием, серезностью и облагораживающей любовью, с какими я выполнил свой труд, я буду вполне вознагражден.

В Пискѣ, 1929 г. *Проф. От. Шевчик*

OT. ŠEVČÍK, op. 17.

STUDIE.

H. Wieniawski 2. Concerto in D-moll / minor

Jeder Bruchteil des Konzertes ist erst dann auszuführen, nachdem vorher alle diesbezüglichen Studien vorgenommen wurden.

Each section of the concerto should be played only, when one has finished its relative study.

On ne doit exécuter chaque section du concerto qu'après avoir achevé tous les exercices en appartenant.

Cada parte del concierto debe ser ejecutada después de haber practicado los estudios correspondientes.

Každý zlomek koncertu budiž hrán teprve tehdy, když byly procvičeny všechny k němu příslušné studie.

Każdą część koncertu można będzie dopiero wtedy odpowiednio oddać, kiedy wykonane zostały odnoszące się do niego studja.

Ogni frammento del concerto non deve essere eseguito che dopo lo studio di tutti gli esercizi che si riferiscomo a quella sezione.

Каждый отрывок концерта исполняется лишь после того, как будут исполнены означенныя буквами упражнения.

Anal.
Fr.
B 15-21
Interv.
Anal.
M.
cresc.

restez
cresc.
Passage B 19-21
mit Stricharten. | with bowings. | avec coups d'archet. | con golpes de arco.
se smyky. | w ćwiczeniach smyczkowych. | con colpi d'arco. | со штриховкой.
sautillé
sautillé

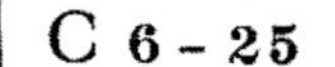

Interv.

C 6 - 19

Anal.

C 20

Oktaventonleiter mit 1., 4. Finger.

Octave - Scales 1st, 4th fingers.

Octaves - gamme avec 1er, et 4ème doigts.

Escalas de octaves con el 1º y 4º dedo.

Oktávové stupnice 1., 4. prstem.

Gamy w oktawach 1., 4. palcem.

Scale di ottave con il 1º, ed il 4º dito.

Гаммы съ 1, 4 пальцами.

*) Der Daumen rückt gleichzeitig in die 2. Lage.
**) Mit gleichem Finger den ganzen Takt.

*) Thumb slides at the same time to the 2nd position.
**) The whole measure with the same finger.

*) Le pouce accompagne la main à la 2ème position.
**) Toute la mesure avec le même doigt.

*) El pulgar acompaña la mano a la 2ª posición.
**) Codo el compás con el mismo dedo.

*) Palec klouže současně do 2. polohy.
**) Celý takt týmž prstem.

*) Wielki palec posuwa się równocześnie do 2. pozycji.
**) Tym samym palcem cały takt.

*) Il pollice ritorna nello stesso tempo nella 2ª posizione.
**) Lo stesso dito per tutta la battuta.

*) Ъольшой палец одновременно скользит во II позицию.
**) Целый такт однимъ и темже пальцемъ.

Zu 4 Noten. | By 4 notes. | Pour le quatre notes. | Para las cuatro notas.
Po 4 notách. | Po 4 nut. | A 4 note. | Для четырех нот.

Oktaven-Tonleiter mit Fingersatz $\frac{1-2}{3-4}$.

Scales in octaves with fingering $\frac{1-2}{3-4}$.

Gammes en octaves doigtées $\frac{1-2}{3-4}$.

Escalas en octavas doigtées $\frac{1-2}{3-4}$.

Stupnice v oktávách s prstokladem $\frac{1-2}{3-4}$.

Gamy w oktawach; opalcowanie $\frac{1-2}{3-4}$.

Scale di ottave diteggiate $\frac{1-2}{3-4}$.

Гаммы съ размещенiем пальцев $\frac{1-2}{3-4}$.

Tonleiter mit verdeckten Oktaven.
Stupnice s krytými oktávami.
Scales in covered octaves.
Gamy z ukrytemi oktawami.
Gammes avec octaves muettes.
Scala di false ottave.
Escalas con octavas mudas.
Группы со скрытыми октавами.
D 1-12
Interv.

D 1-2
Anal.
D 3-8
M.
Sp.
Fr.

Fr.
Sp.
M.
Fr.
D 9 - 12
Interv.
Anal.
Fr.
Sp.

*) Zuerst fest, um d. Platz für Flageolett zu finden.

**) Während d. Gleitens zum Flageolett wird d. 2. Finger nach u. nach ausgestreckt.

*) Zprvu pevný hmat nechť určí místo pro flageolet.

**) V posouvání ku flageoletu budiž 2. prst pozvolna napínán.

*) Firstly the pressed finger to fix the place for the harmonic.

**) In sliding to harmonic, the 2nd finger should be gradually extended.

*) Naprzód silnie przycisnąć palcem, aby znaleść miejsce pewne dla flageolettu.

**) Podczas gdy wysuwamy palec na flageolett, drugi palec stopniowo, coraz więcej wydłuża się.

*) Pour trouver la place exacte de l'harmonique, appuyer le doigt.

**) En glissant vers l'harmonique, le 2ème doigt s'étire peu à peu.

*) Dapprima premere il dito per trovare il posto dell armonico.

**) Durante il portamento dei suoni armonici bisogna distendere di più in più il 2º dito.

*) Para encontrar el sitio exacto del enharmónico apoyar el dedo con firmeza.

**) Al deslizarse hacia el enharmónico, el 2º dedo se extiende poco a poco.

*) Сначала сильный нажим, чтобы определить место для flageoletto.

**) Во время скольжения к flageoletto второй палецъ постепенно натягивается.

Passage D 1 - 2

mit 35 Stricharten.
s 35 smyky.

with 35 bowings.
z 35 ćwiczeniami smyczkowemi.

avec 35 coups d'archet.
con 35 colpi d'arco.

con 35 golpes de arco.
с 35 видами штриховки.

*) Bei Ausführung der Stricharten sind die Vortragszeichen genau zu beachten.

*) V provedení jednotlivých smyků jest nutno přesně dbáti přednesových znamének.

*) In executing bowings it is necessary to observe the interpretive signs.

*) Przy wykonaniu smyczkowych ćwiczeń musimy dokladną uwagę zwrócić na oznaczenia interpretacyjne.

*) Il faut observer rigoureusement les signes d'interprétation pour l'exécution des coups d'archet.

*) Nell' eseguire i colpi d'arco bisogna osservare esattamente i segni dell interpretazione.

*) Es preciso observar rigurosamente los signos de interpretación para la ejecución de los golpes de arco.

*) При исполнении штриховки не забывать на выразительность.

cresc.
dim.
Sp.
Fr.
M.
spiccato
sautillé
D 13 - 18
Interv.
III.

D 13 - 14

D 15 - 16
a)
M.
III
Fr.
Sp.
Passage
D 13 - 14
mit 9 Stricharten. | with 9 bowings. | avec 9 coups d' archet. | con 9 golpes de arco.
s 9 smyky. | z 9 ćwiezeniami smyczkowemi. | con 9 colpi d' arco. | с 9 видами штриховки.
cresc.
dim.
ricochet

b)
mp
cresc.
f
dim.
Sp.
Fr.
M.
ricochet
(werfen, jeté.)
D 17 - 18
III.
II.
I.
mf
sf
p
cresc.

*) Treffübung: Die Finger verlassen das Griffbrett, um wieder aufgesetzt zu werden, der Bogen bleibt während der Pause auf der Saite.

*) For surety of the left hand: The hand leaves the fingerboard to be replaced again, but the bow must rest on the string during this process.

*) Exercice de changement de position sans point d'appui: L'archet reste placé sur les cordes pendant les silences, tandis que les doigts quittant la touche, se replacent sur la corde.

*) Ejercicio de cambio de posición sin punto de apoyo: El arco queda sobre las cuerdas durante los silencios, mientras los dedos dejan el diapasón y se vuelven a colocar sobre la cuerda.

*) Cvičení dopadu: Prsty opouštějí hmatník, aby pak opětně na tento byly postaveny. Smyčec však v pomlce zůstává na struně.

*) Ćwiczenia w trafianiu tonów. Palce wypuszczają szyjkę i powracają znowu na to same miejsce, smyczek zaś pozostaje w czasie pauzy na strunie.

*) Esercizi per afferrare le posizioni alte: I diti lasciano la tastiera per essere di nuovo collocati lasciando l'arco sulla corda durante la pausa.

*) Упражнения в перемене позиции без опоры: Все пальцы оставляют шейку, чтобы по паузе вновь упасть на нее. Смычок же и в паузе остается на струне.

D 23 - 24

E 1 - 26
Interv.
E 1 - 14
Anal.
E 15 - 26
Interv.

*) Zuerst fest. | *) Firm at first. | *) D'abord fermement. | *) Primero con firmeza. | *) Napřed pevně hmatati.
*) Najpierw silnie przycisnąć palcami. | *) Dapprima premere il dito. | *) Сначала сильный нажим.

IV.
Fr.
IV
mp
Fr.
Sp.
p
F 26 - 27
mf
f
mp

Passage F 24 - 27

mit 11 Stricharten. | with 11 bowings. | avec 11 coups d'archet. | con 11 golpes de arco.
s 11 smyky. | 11 ćwiczeniami smyczkowemi. | con 11 colpi d'arco. | с 11 видами штриховки.

F 28

Anal.

F 29
mp
f
p
mf
cresc.
Fr.
Sp.
II

F 30 - 31
mf
sf
p
f
Passage F 28 - 31
mit 9 Stricharten. | with 9 bowings. | avec 9 coups d'archet. | con 9 golpes de arco.
s 9 smyky. | 9 ćwiczeniami smyczkowemi. | con 9 colpi d'arco. | с 9 видами штриховки.
IV
Sp.
Fr.
spiccato
G 5 - 9
Interv.
II
III
mp
IV
I

Anal.
mf
f
mf
f
mf
f
f
mf
f
sf
mp
a)
b)

mp

Passage
G 5-9
mit Stricharten. | with bowings. | avec coups d'archet. | con golpes de arco.
se smyky. | z ćwiczeniami smyczkowemi. | con colpi d'arco. | со штриховкой.
G 10-11
sempre f

G 12-13

Chromatische Rückungen im Umfang einer kleiner Terz, reinen Quarte und Quinte.

Chromatická posouvaní v rozsahu malé tercie, čisté kvarty a kvinty.

Proceed chromatically to the extent of a diminished third, perfect fourth and fifth.

Chromatyczne posunięcia w obrębie małej tercji, czystej kwarty i kwinty.

Mouvements chromatiques. (Tierce mineure, quarte juste, quinte juste.)

Ritorno cromatico d'intervalli di una terza minore e di una quarta e quinta giusta.

Movimientos cromáticos. Tercera menor, cuarta justa, quinta justa.

Хроматическия движения в границах малой терции, чистой кварты и квинты.

*)Im Heruntergleiten von der 5. Lage rückt der Daumen mit.

*)V sestupné výměně z 5. polohy klouže palec současně.

*)By gliding downwards from the fifth position, the thumb moves along also.

*)W pochodach w dół od piątej pozycji posuwa się wielki palec razem z ręką.

*)Dans la descente de la cinquième position, le pouce glisse en même temps que les autres doigts.

*)Discendendo dalla 5º posizione il pollice discende insieme.

*)Para bajar de la quinta posición, el pulgar se desliza al mismo tiempo que los otros dedos.

*)При движении вниз из 5 позиции большой палец скользит одновременно.

Von der 3. Lage zur 12.Lage.

Z 3. polohy do 12.

From the third position to the 12th position.

Od 3 do 12 pozycji.

De la 3ème position à la 12ème position.

Dalla 3ª alla 12ª posizione.

De la 3ª posición a la 12ª posición.

Съ III позиции въ XIIую.

Glissando mittels Tremolo des 3. Fingers.

Glissando vykonané tremolem (vibratem) 3. prstu.

Glissando by means of tremolo of the 3rd finger.

Glissando zapomocą tremola trzeciego palca.

Glissando moyennant le tremolo du 3éme doigt.

Glissando del 3º dito per mezzo del tremolo.

Glissando tremblante del 3.dedo.

Glissando с помощью тремоло 3 пальца.

*) Gleiten ohne Tremolo (keine bestimmten Töne, Takt einhalten.)

**) Das Tremolo vorbereiten und

***) tremolierend heruntergleiten.

*) Klouzati bez tremola (žádné určité tóny, dodržeti takt.)

**) Připraviti tremolo a

***) v tremolu sklouznouti.

*) Glissando without tremolo - No definite notes - time to be kept of the bar.

**) The tremolo to be prepared and

***) during tremolo glide downwards.

*) Glissando bez tremola (nieoznaczone tony, utrzymać takt.)

**) Przygotować tremolo i

***) tremclując cofać rękę w dół.

*) Glissando sans vibrato, sans préoccupation de note définie - mais en maintenant la mesure.

**) Commencer le vibrato,

***) puis descendre en glissant avec vibrato.

*) Glissando senza tremolo (senza suoni determinati, ma osservando il ritmo.)

**) Preparare il tremolo e

***) discendere tremolando.

*) Glisando sin vibrato, sin preocupación de notas determinadas, pero conservando el compás.

**) Empezar el vibrato,

***) después bajar glisando con vibrato.

*) Скольженіе без tremolo (без определенного тона, темп сохранить.)

**) Приготовить tremolo и

***) таким способом соскользнуть.

senza trem.
con trem.
senza vibrato
vibrato e gliss.
H 1 - 18
Interv.
cres - - - - - - - - cen - - - - - - - do

*) facilité

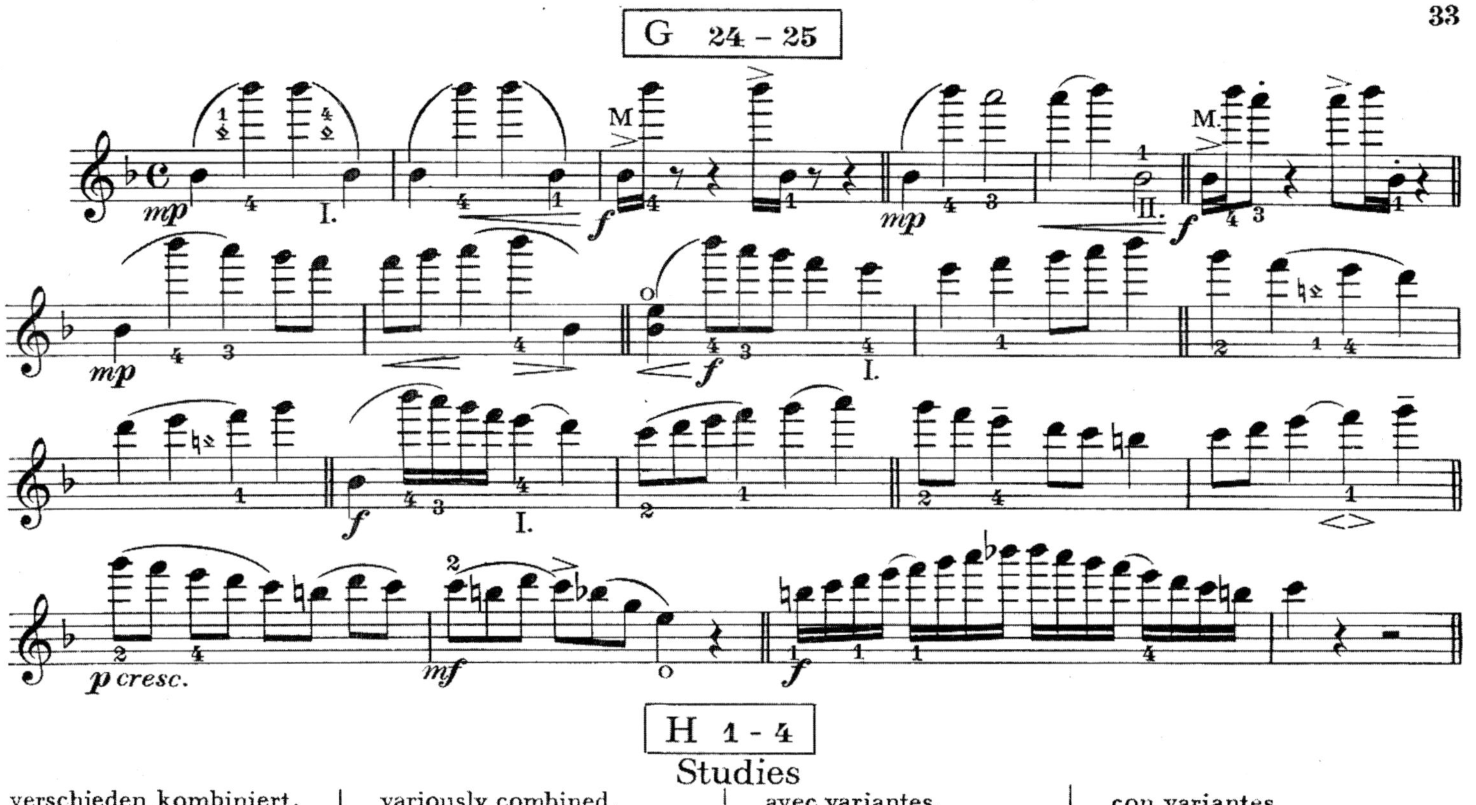

H 1 - 4

Studies

verschieden kombiniert. | variously combined. | avec variantes. | con variantes.
různě kombinované. | w różnych kombinacjach. | variamente combinati. | различно составленныя.

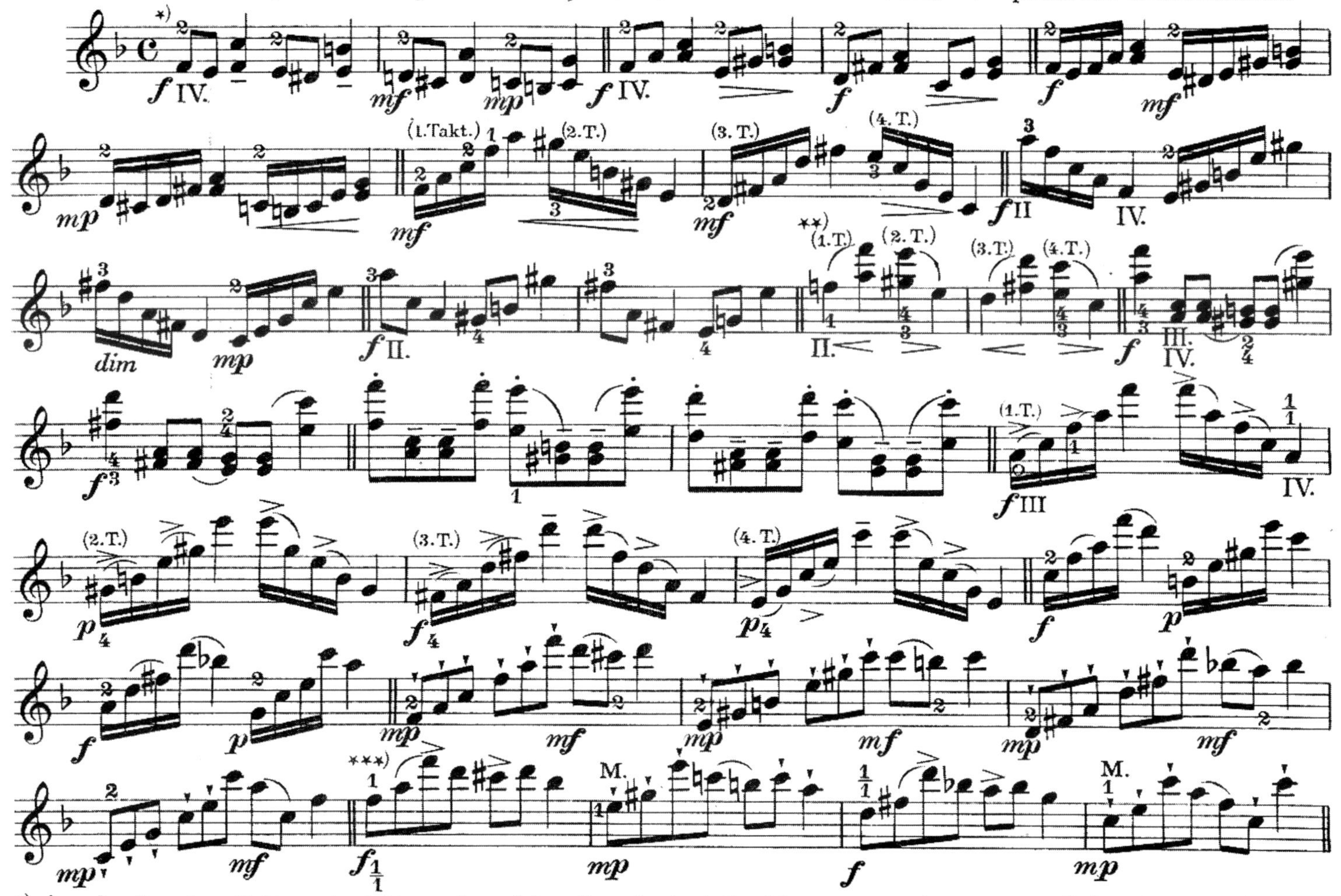

(1.Takt.) (2.T.) (3.T.) (4.T.)

*) Aus den 4 ersten Takten der 1. Taktteil allein.

**) Der 2. Taktteil allein.

***) Der 3. und 4. Taktteil.

*) Ze čtyř prvých taktů pouze 1. taktová skupina.

**) Pouze 2. taktová skupina.

***) 3. a 4. taktová skupina.

*) From the 1st four bars the 1st part of the bar.

**) The second part of the bar.

***) The third and fourth part of the bar.

*) Z początkowych czterech taktów, tylko pierwsza część taktu.

**) Druga część taktu.

***) Trzecia i czwarta część taktu.

*) Seul, le 1er temps des 4 premières mesures.

**) Seul, le 2ème temps.

***) Seul, le 3ème temps le 4ème temps.

*) Delle prime 4 misure solo la prima battuta della misura.

**) Solo la 2a parte della misura.

***) La 3a e la 4a parte della misura.

*) Solo, el primer tiempo de los cuatro primeros compases.

**) Solo, el segundo tiempo.

***) Solo, el tercer tiempo el cuarto tiempo.

*) Из первых 4 тактов лишь I четверть.

**) Лишь IIю четверть.

***) Лишь III и IVю четверть.

*) Der 1. und 4. Taktteil aus den vier ersten Takten.
*) 1. a 4. taktová skupina z prvých 4 taktů.

*) The 1st and 4th part of bar out of the 4 first bars.
*) Pierwsza i czwarta część taktu z początkowych czterech taktów.

*) Le 1er et 4ème temps des 4 premières mesures.
*) La 1a e la 4a parte della misura delle prime 4 misure.

*) El 1º y 4º tiempo de los cuatro primeros compases.
*) I и IVю четверть 4 первых тактов.

Passage **G 24-25**

mit Staccato - Stricharten.
se staccatovými smyky.

with staccato bowing styles.
ćwiczeniami smyczkowemi „staccato.“

avec „Staccato.“
con colpi d'arco „staccato.“

con Staccato.
стакатовой штриховкой.

Passage **G 24-25, H 1 - 9**

mit verschiedenen Stricharten.
s různými smyky.

with various bowing styles.
różne ćwiczenia smyczkowe.

avec différents coups d'archet.
con differenti colpi d'arco.

con diferentes golpes de arco.
разной штриховкой.

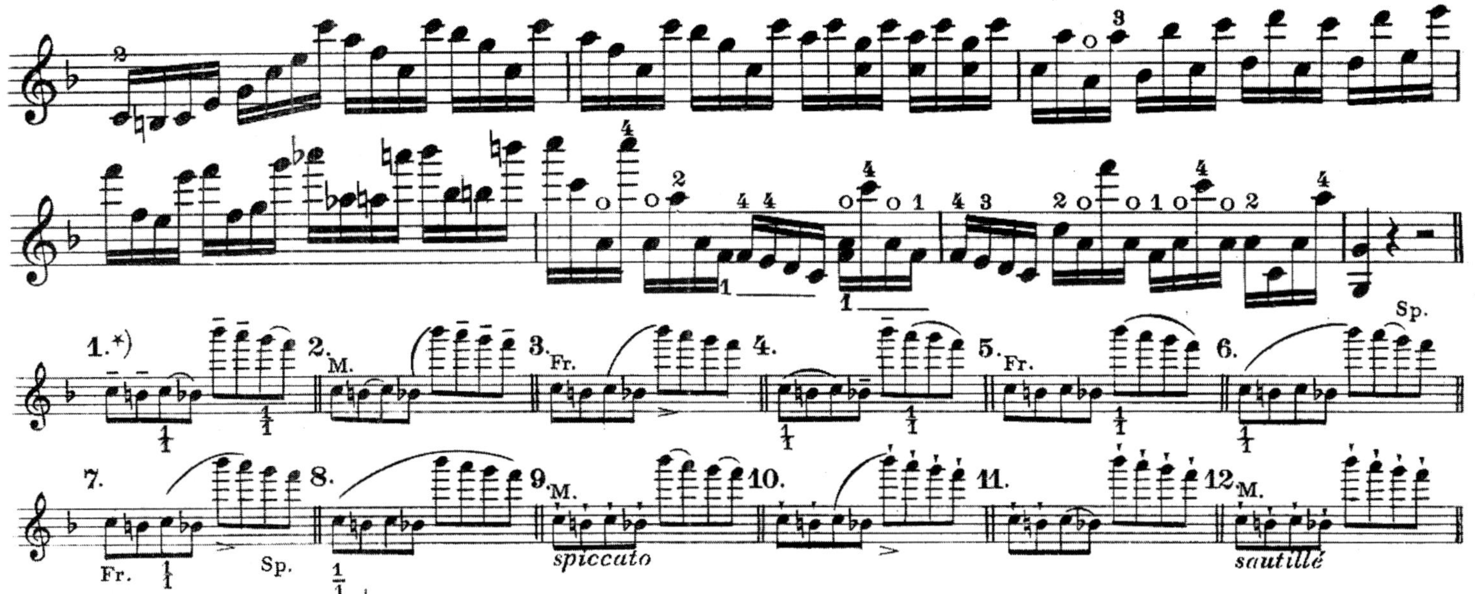

*) Die Stricharten im langsameren Tempo auszuführen.

*) Smyky nutno cvičiti ve volnějším tempu.

*) The bowing styles to be performed in slow tempo.

*) Ćwiczenia smyczkowe wykonywać w wolniejszem tempie.

*) Il faut exécuter plus lentement le mouvement des coups d'archet.

*) Suonare i colpi d'arco in tempo più lento.

*) Es preciso ejecutar más lentamente el movimiento de los golpes de arco.

*) Штриховка в медленном темпе.

H 10 – 18

Interv.

H 10 – 11

Anal.

mf pp mf p f
pp mp p mf p
mp pp mf

*) Absteigend mit demselben Fingersatz wie aufsteigend. **) Jeder Takt vermehrt um einen Ton verschieden rhythmysiert.	*) While descending with same fingering as ascending. **) To each bar add another, the tone to be rhythmically varied.	*) Le même doigté en montant et en descendant. **) Chaque mesure accrue d'un son, mais rythmée différemment.	*) El mismo doigté subiendo y bajando. **) Cada compás aumentado de un sonido, pero ritmado diferentemente.
*) Sestupmo s týmž prstokladem jako vzestupmo. **) Každý takt znmožen o jeden tón, různě rytmisován.	*) W pochodach w górę i w dół to samo opalcowanie. **) Każdy takt powiększony o jeden ton rozmaicie rytmowany.	*) Discendere e salire con la stessa diteggiatura. **) Scomporre ogni misura aggiungendo ogni volta una nota e cambiandone il ritmo.	*) При подъеме та же разстановка как и при спуску. **) К каждому такту прибавляется один тон ритмически разный.

mit anderem Fingersatz. s jiným prstokladem.	with different fingering. inne opalcowanie.	avec d'autres doigtés. con un' altra diteggiatura.	con otros doigtés. с другой разстановкой пальцев.

b) p
a) f

13

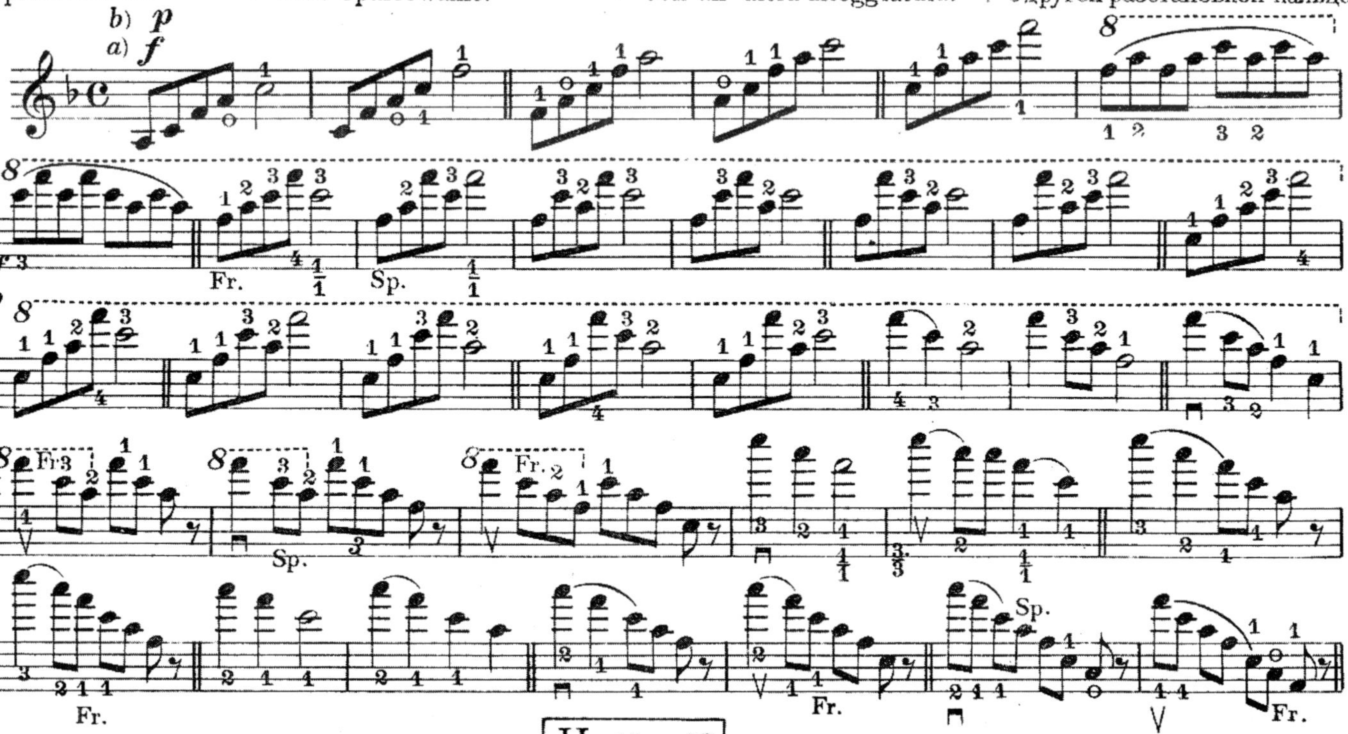

a) f
b) p

Fr. Sp. Fr. Sp. Fr. Sp. Fr. Fr. Fr. Sp. Fr.

H 14 - 18

p poco a poco cresc. p cresc.

p segue cresc. f

Ammerkung: Nicht nur das Einüben einer Passage, sondern auch eines Vortragsstückes soll in kleinen Gruppen erfolgen und die Phrasierung, Nuancierung und Interpretation auf Bruchteilen der Melodie versucht werden, um die Reproduktion des Musikstückes nicht der Willkür der momentanen Eingebung zu überlassen.

Note: Not only should the passages be exercised but also at the same time, the exercises of a smaller piece should follow in little groups, and the phrasing nuances and interpretation should be tried at in parts of a melody so that the execution of the piece should not be left to the will of a momentary suggestion.

Observation: Ce n'est pas seulement dans les passages brillants, mais aussi dans les phrases mélodiques qu'il convient de travailler d'une façon fragmentée par petits groupes de notes; et cela, tout en respectant la loi du phrasé et de la nuance, pour ne pas abandonner l'éxecution du morceau à la seule inspiration du moment.

Observación: No es sólo en los pasajes brillantes sino también en las frases melódicas que conviene trabajar de una manera fragmentaria, en pequeños grupos de notas; y eso siémpre respetando las leyes del fraseado y del matiz, para no abandonar la ejecución de la pieza a la sola inspiración del momento.

Poznámka: Nejen jednotlivé pasáže, ale i skladbu přednesovou jest nutno cvičiti v menších skupinách a pokoušeti se o frazování, nuancování a interpretaci zlomků melodie, aby reprodukce dotyčné skladby nebyla ponechána libovůli okamžité nálady.

Uwaga: Nietylko ćwiczenie poszczególnych pasaży lecz także całego utworu ma się odbywać w małych grupach a frazowanie, nuanse i interpretacja powinne być wykonane na małych częściach melodji aby odtworzenie utworu muzycznego nie ulegało wpływom samowoli chwilowego natchnienia.

Osservazione: Non solamente i passaggi brillanti ma auche le frasi melodiche vanno studiate a piccoli gruppi di note sempre rispettando l'interpretazione ed i coloriti per non abbondonare l'esecuzione del pezzo allo stato d'animo del momento.

Чтобы репродукция музыкальной вещи не зависела от случайностей вашего настроения, нужно, как при исполнении пассажей, так и отдельных отрывков мелодии, преследовать фразировку, нюансы и трактовку их.

ROMANCE.

Andante non troppo.

1 - 8

*) Takt 1-2 in verschiedener Abstufung. Im 1. Takt soll in der Begleitung die 2. Triole des Rhythmus wegen betont werden.

**) Am Ende des Taktes anschwellen, um das folgende *f* vorzubereiten.

*) Bar 1-2 in various gradations. In the 1st bar in the accompaniment the 2nd triplet should be accentuated on account of the rhythm.

**) At the end of the bar crescendo to prepare the following *f*.

*) Mesure 1-2 nuances différentes. Dans l'accompagnement, il faut accentuer le 2ème triolet de la 1ère mesure à cause du rythme.

**) A la fin de la mesure, intensifier pour préparer le *f* qui suit.

*) Compas 1-2 matices diferentes. En el acompañamiento, hay que acentuar el 2º tresillo del 1er compás a causa del ritmo.

**) Al final del compás intensificar para preparar el *f* que sigue.

*) 1.-2. takt v různém odstupňování. Pro ostré vyhranění rytmu budiž v doprovodu zdůrazněna v 1. taktu 2. triola.

**) Sesilovati již ku konci taktu k přípravě následujího *f*.

*) Takt 1-2 w różnem stopniowaniu. Przy akompaniamencie, w takcie 1. musi być drugi triol dla utzymania rytmu wyraźnie zaakcentowany.

**) Przy końcu taktu wzmocnić crescendo dla przygotowania następującego *f*.

*) La misura 1-2 in differenti gradazioni discendenti. La 2º terzina della 1ª misura deve essere fortemente accentuata dall' accompagnamento a causa del ritmo.

**) Alla fine della misura cominciare il crescendo per preparare il forte che segue.

*) I и II такты различно оттененные. Ради ритма в I такте II триоль в аккомпанименте должна быть подчеркнута.

**) Усилить уже в конце такта чтобы приготовить идущее дальше forte.

*) Diese Phrase herausheben, um vom Orchester nicht erdrückt zu werden.
**) Mit Leidenschaft.
***) *pp*, als Kontrast zum Anfang der Romanze.

+) Mit schmetterdem Ton, nahe am Steg.
++) Mit liegendem Bogen, geschoben und nett abgesondert.
+++) Sehr zart.
⊕) Die Halbe heftig attakkieren.

*) This phrase well out, so as not to get crushed (drowned) by the orchestra.
**) With passion.
***) Pianissimo as a contrast to the beginning of the Romance.
+) With dashing tone, near the bridge.
++) With lying bow, detached and smartly separated.

+++) Very delicately.
⊕) The breve to be violently attacked.

*) Faire ressortir cette phrase afin de ne pas être dominé par l'orchestre.
**) Avec passion.
***) *pp*. pour contraster avec le commencement de la Romance.
+) Avec un son vigoureux l'archet à la corde.

++) L'archet sur la corde, les notes distinctement séparées.

+++) Très doux.
⊕) Forte attaque de la blanche.

*) Hacer resaltar esta frase para no ser dominado por la orquesta.
**) Con pasión.
***) *pp*. para marcar el contraste con el principio de la Romanza.
+) Con un sonido vigoroso el arco a la cuerda.

++) Con arco leyendo, resbalando y tierno y apartado.

+++) Muy suave.
⊕) Ataque fuerte de la blanca.

*) Výrazně zahráti tuto frázi, aby orchestrem nebyla zastíněna.
**) Vášnivě.
***) *pp*, kontrastující s počátkem Romance.
+) S hřmotně pronikavým tónem blíže kobylky.
++) S ležícím smyčcem, plíživě a něžně oddělováno.

+++) Velmi jemně.
⊕) Půlovou notu prudce naraziti (atakovati.)

*) Przy tem zdaniu ton wzmocnić, aby nie zostać przytłumionym przes orkiestrę.
**) namiętnie.
***) *pp* jak kontrast do początku romancy.
+) Druzgocącym tonem blizko podstawki.
++) Leżącym smyczkiem, każdy ton delikatnie odosobńiony.
+++) Bardzo delikatnie.
⊕) Półnuty silnie atakować.

*) Questa frase deve essere fatta risaltare perchè non sia coperta dall'orchestra.
**) Con passione.
***) *pp* per il contrasto del principio della Romanza.
+) Con sonorità vicino al ponticello
++) Con l'arco alla corda con lo staccato bene tenuto e separato.
+++) Dolcissimo.
⊕) Attaccare fortemente la minima.

*) Эту фразу играть выразительно, чтобы она не была задавлена оркестром.
**) Страстно
***) *pp*, как контраст с началом Романса.
+) Гремучим тоном, у кобылки.
++) Съ лежащим смычком, осторожно скользя и нежно отделяя.
+++) Очень нежно.
⊕) Половинные ноты ръзко обозначать.

*) Scharf betonen.
**) Détaché aus der Schulter.

*) Accentuate sharply.
**) Détaché from the shoulder.

*) Vigoureusement accentué.
**) Détaché de l'épaule.

*) Vigorosamente acentuado.
**) Détaché del hombro.

*) Ostře zdůrazniti.
**) Détaché z nadloktí.

*) Ostro akcentować.
**) Détaché akcentowane z ramienia.

*) Accentuato fortemente.
**) Détaché della spalla.

*) С острым ударением.
**) Посыл смычка от плеча (целой рукой-detaché)

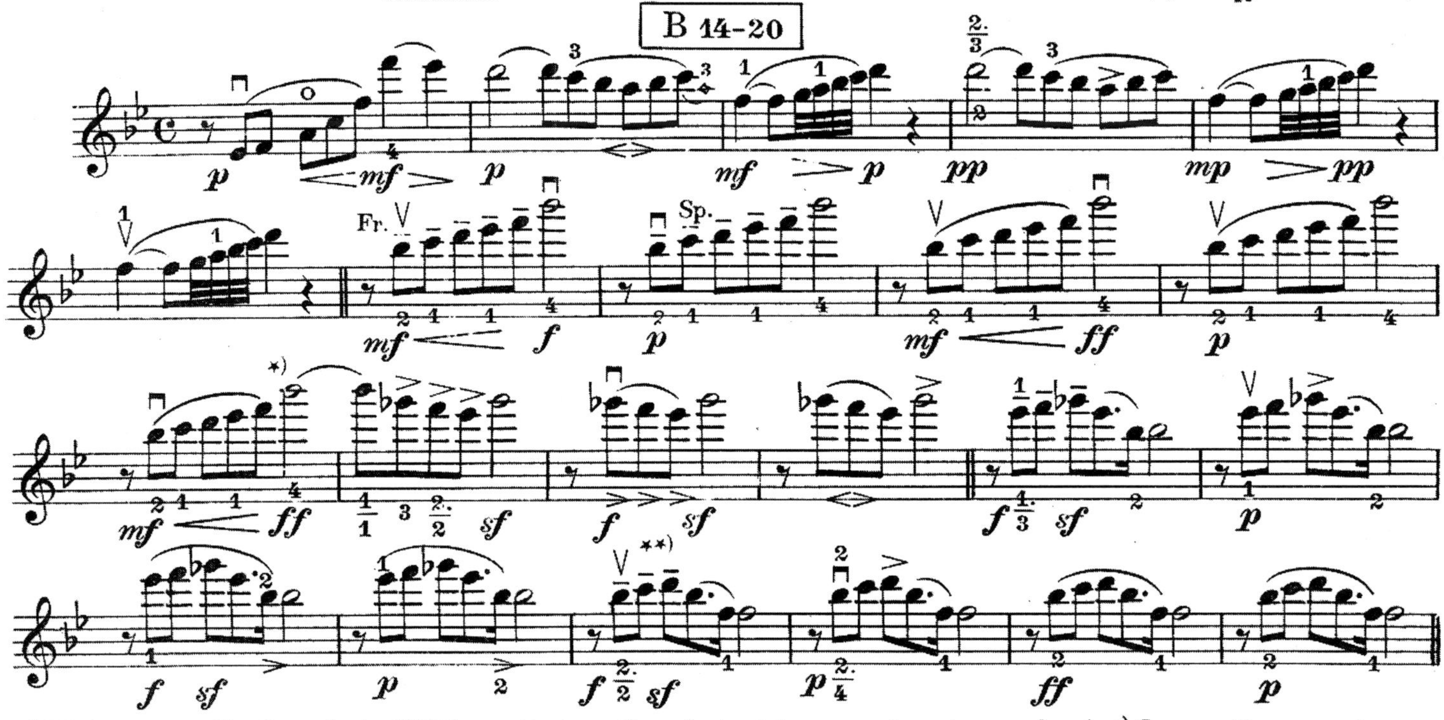

*) Mit grösster Kraft und Leidenschaft.
**) Heftig herausgestossen.

*) With great strength and passion.
**) Violently pushed with bow.

*) Avec passion et avec la plus grande puissance.
**) En grand détaché.

*) Con pasión y con el mayor vigor.
**) En gran détaché.

*) S největší silou a vášní.
**) Prudce akcentováno.

*) Z największą werwą i uczuciem.
**) Gwałtownie akcentować.

*) Con la più grande forza e passione.
**) Con un arco détaché.

*) С большой силой и страстью.
**) С сильным ударением.

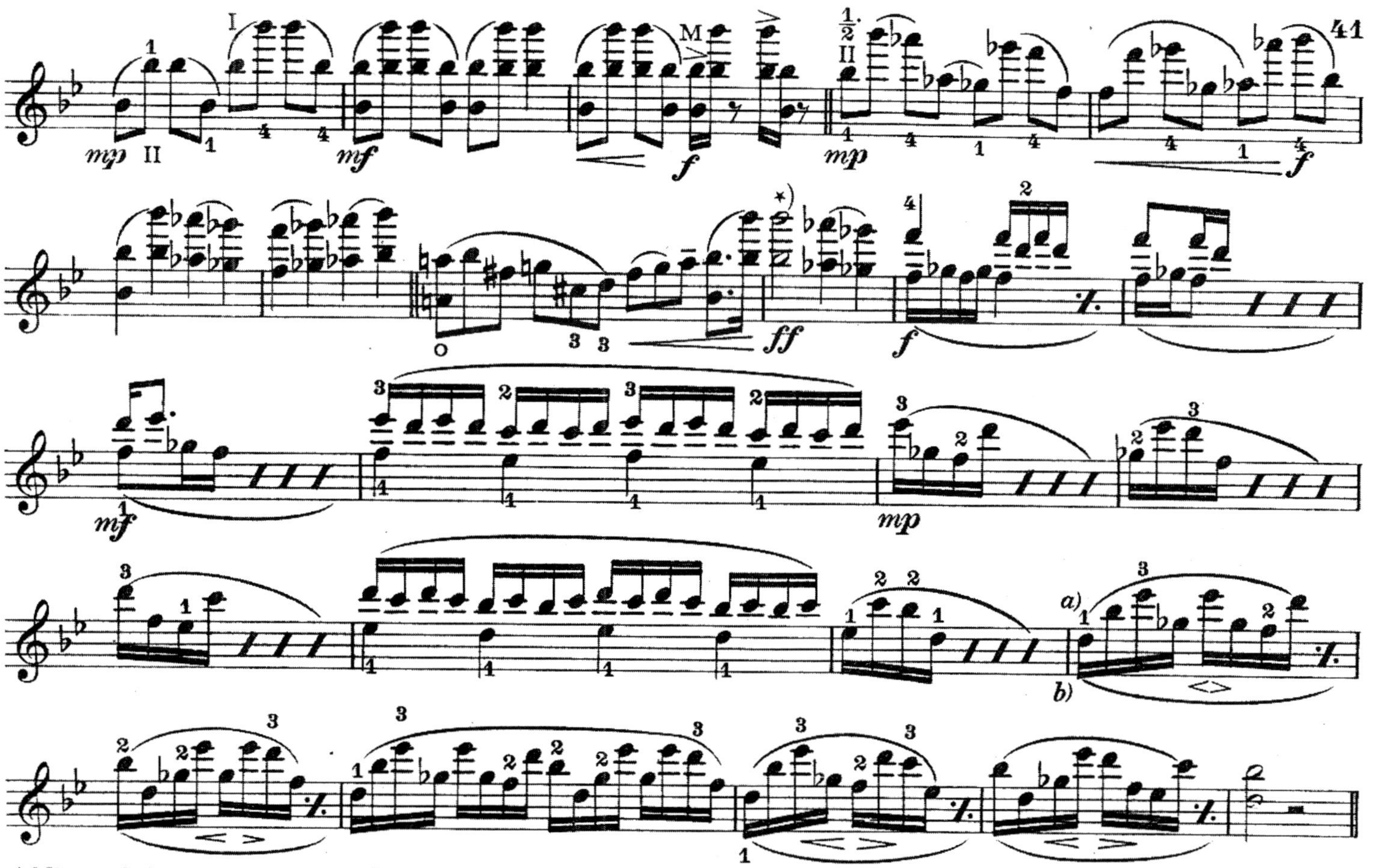

*) Mit mächtigem Ton, nahe am Steg.

*) With mighty tone, near the bridge.

*) Avec un son fort et puissant, près du chevalet.

*) Con un sonido fuerte y poderoso cerca del puente.

*) mocným tónem, blíže kobylky.

*) Potężnym tonem, blizko podstawki.

*) Con suono possente vicino al ponticello.

*) Могучим тоном, у кобылки.

C 3 - 13

Più mosso. *a tempo*

ritard.

a tempo

D 3-11

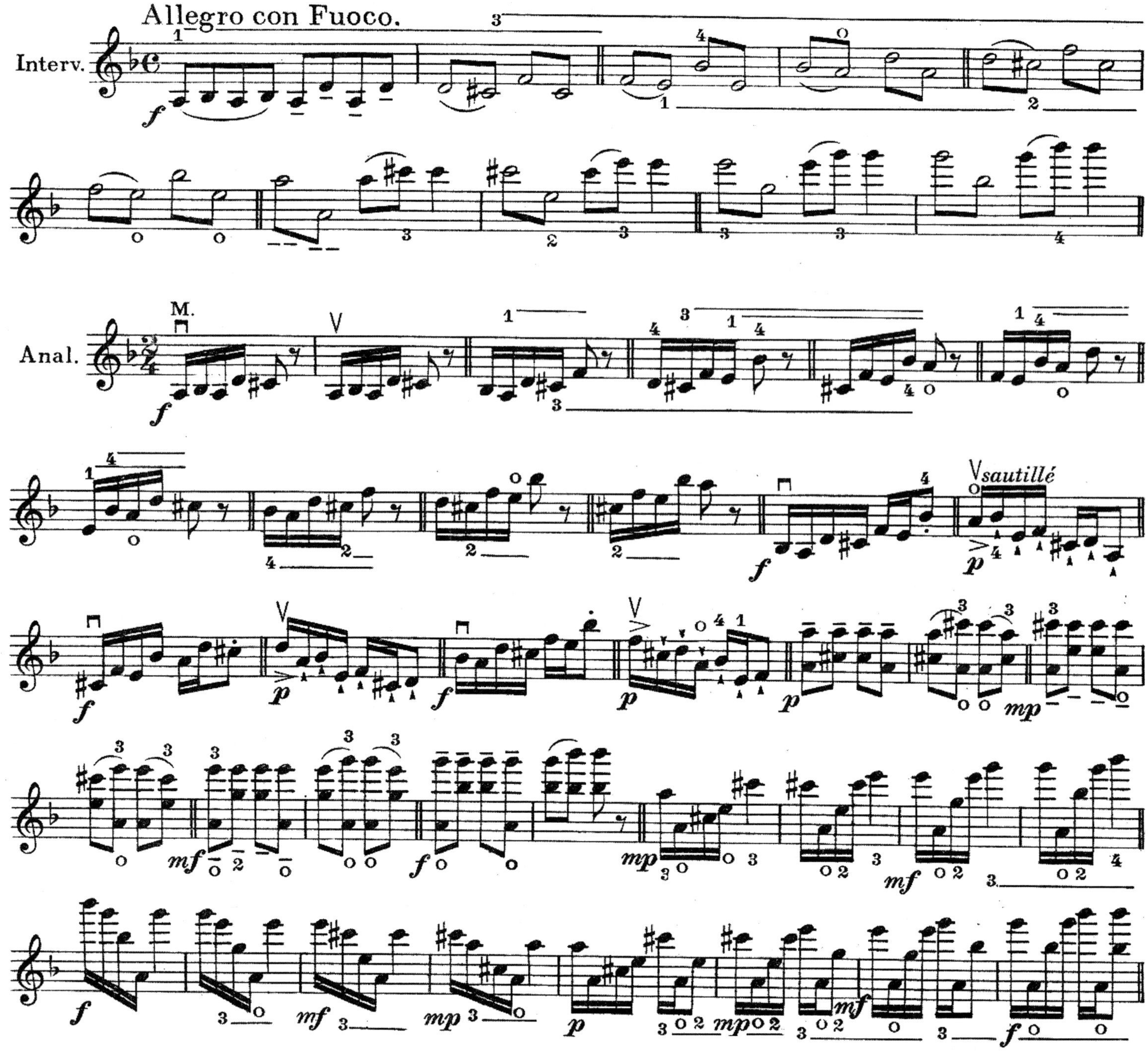
Allegro con Fuoco.
Interv.
Anal.
sautillé

Passage mit 8 Veränderungen des Bogenstriches

Passage with 8 bowing variations.

Passage avec 8 variations de coups d'archet.

Pasaje con 8 variantes de golpes de arco.

Pasáž s 8 změnami smyku.

Pasaż z 8 różnemi ćwiczeniami smyczkowemi.

Passaggio con 8 cambiamenti di colpi d'arco.

Пассажи с 8 разными штриховками.

Moderato.
cresc.
Fr.
Allegro.
M.sautillé

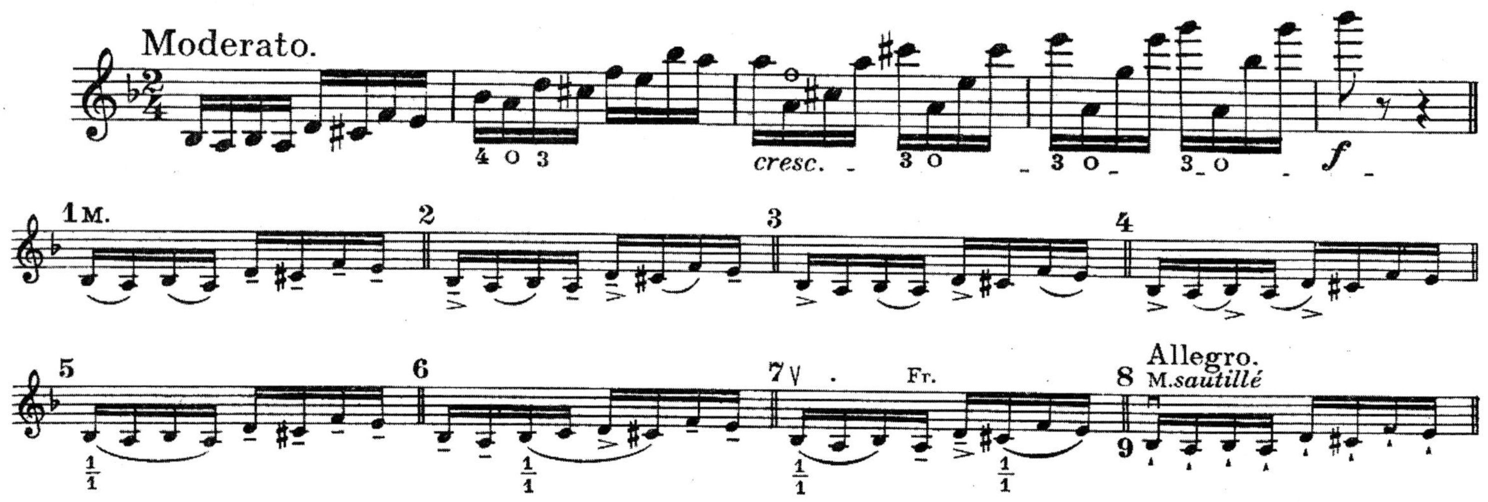

*) Beim Wiederholen mit springendem Bogen ohne die für détaché bezeichneten Stricharten.

*) At the repetition with hopping bow without the bowing styles marked détaché.

*) Lors de la 2ème reprise, faire tout en sautillé excepter des notes indiquées à faire en détaché.

*) En la 2ª repetición, hágase todo en saltillo, exceptuando las notas indicadas en détaché.

*) Při opakování se smyčcem skákavým bez smyků označených pro détaché.

*) Przy powtórzeniu skaczącym smyczkiem bez oznaczonych „détaché"smyczków.

*) Nel ripetere suonare spiccato. Senza i colpi d'arco scritti per lo staccato.

*) При повторении скачущей штриховкой, без штрихов détaché.

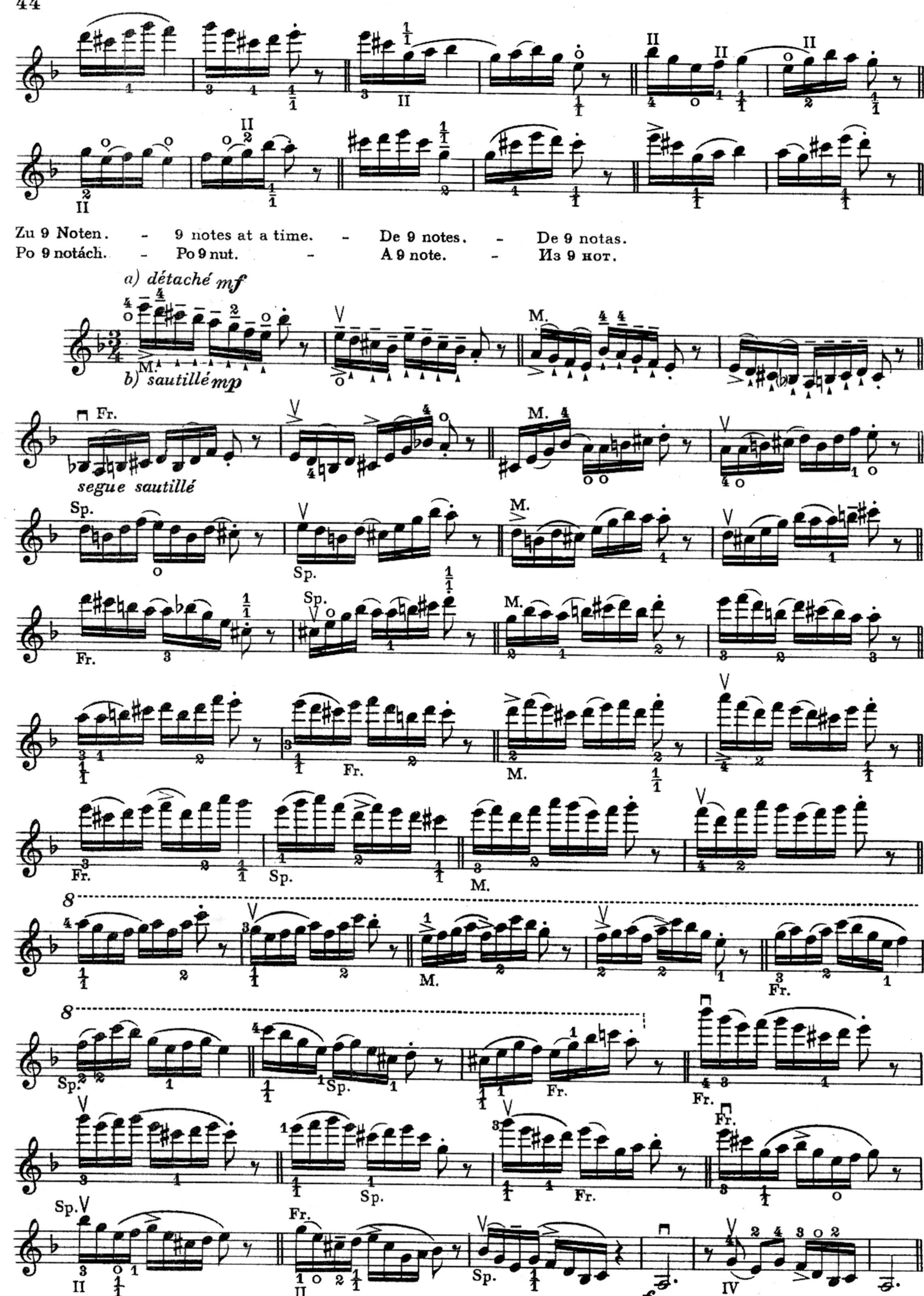
Zu 9 Noten. - 9 notes at a time. - De 9 notes. - De 9 notas.
Po 9 notách. - Po 9 nut. - A 9 note. - Из 9 нот.
a) détaché mf
b) sautillé mp
segue sautillé

Passage mit 15 Veränderungen des Bogenstriches.
Pasáž s 15 změnami smyku.

Passage with 15 bowing variations.
Pasaż z 15 różnemi ćwiczeniami smyczkowemi.

Passage avec 15 variations de coups d'archet.
Passaggio con 15 cambiamenti di colpi d'arco.

Pasaje con 15 variantes de golpes de arco.
Пассажи с 15 разными штриховками.

f p mp mf f II

1 Fr. 2 Sp. 3 4 5 6 M.
7 Fr. 8 Sp. 9 Fr. Sp. 10 Fr. 11 M *spiccato* 12 M.
13 M. 14 M. *sautillé* 15

III.

A 3 - 22

Allegro. (♩ = 116-120) *(A la Zingara)*

Interv.

mf f mp p

A 3 – 16

*) Beim Spiccato wird die erste Note geworfen, das sautille (schnell springend aus dem Handgelenk) beginnt dagegen liegend, erst nach der 2. Note springt der Bogen auf.

*) At the spiccato the first note is thrown, on the other hand, the sautillé (quickly rebounding bow from the wrist,) starts with the bow on the strings, only after the second note should the bow jump off.

*) Pour le spiccato, la 1ére note est jetée. Pour le sautillé qui se produit par le mouvement rapide du poignet; il faut, au contraire, que la 1ére note soit faite par l'archet posé. C'est seulement à la 2éme note que l'archet se souléve.

*) Para el spiccato la 1ª nota es jetée. Para el saltillo, que se produce con un movimiento rápido de la muñeca, es preciso al contrario que la 1ª nota se ejecute con el arco a la cuerda. Sólo a la 2ª nota se levanta el arco.

*) Ve spiccatu dostává se první notě úhozu, sautillé naopak (rychle skákavě ze zápěstí) začíná v poloze smyčce ležícího, který teprve při 2. notě skáče.

*) Przy spiccato pierwsza nuta rzucona. Przy sautillé (szybko ruszając przegubem ręki) zaczyna się leżącym smykiem, dopiero po 2 nucie smyczek skacze.

*) Per lo spiccato la 1ª nota deve essere gettata, e il saltellato bisogna eseguirlo presto con il polso ma al contrario l'arco incomincia a saltellare dopo la 2ª nota.

*) При spiccato I нота с ударом, при sautillé (быстро подталкивая запястьем) наоборот: начинаем лежащим смычком и лишь по II ноте смычок подскакивает.

A 17 – 30

Zu 9 Noten mit verschiedenen Bogenstrichen.
To be practised 9 notes at a time with various bowings.
Pour 9 notes avec coups d'archet divers.
Para 9 notas con diversos golpes de arco.
Po 9 notách s různými smyky.
Po 9 nut odmiennymi smyczkami.
A 9 note con differenti colpi d'arco.
9 нотныя группы с различными ходами смычка.
A 11 - 25
a) détaché mf
b) sautillé mp
segue sautillé
Fr.
Sp.
mf
mp
II.

Fr.
Sp.
Dasselbe zu 3 Takten mit springenden Bogen (sautillé.)
The same to be practised 3 bars at a time with hopping bow (sautillé.)
La même, pour 3 mesures du coup d'archet en sautillé.
La misma, para 3 compases del golpe de arco en saltillo.
Totéž ve skupinách po 3 taktech se smyčcem skákavým (sautillé.)
To samo ćwiczyć po trzy takty skaczącym smyczkiem (sautillé.)
Lo stesso a 3 battute con colpo d'arco spiccato (saltellato.)
То же самое въ 3 тактахъ при скачущей штриховке (sautillé)
a)
b)

A 31 - 42

Interv.

A 31 - 36

sautillé
in Doppelgriffen.
with double-stoppings.
en doubles cordes.
en dobles cuerdas.
ve dvojhmatech.
ćwiczenie w akordach.
in doppie corde.
двойной нажим (гриф).
A 37-42
cresc.
Sp.
dim.

A 37 - 42
Fortsetzung der Doppelgriffe.
Continuation of the double stoppings.
Continuation des doubles cordes.
Continuación de las dobles cuerdas.
Pokračování dvojhmatů.
Ciąg dalszy ćwiczeń w podwójnych tonach.
Continuazione delle doppie corde.
Продолжение двойного нажима.
cresc.
dim.
Passage
A 11 - 42
mit 30 Stricharten.
with 30 bowing variations.
avec 30 variantes de coups d'archet.
con 30 variantes de golpes de arco.
s 30 změnami smyku.
wykonać 30 różnemi ćwiczeniami smyczkowemi.
con 30 combiamenti di colpi d'arco.
с 30 разными штриховками.

cresc - cen - do
spiccato
spiccato
sautillé
A 68 - 93
Meno mosso.

cresc.
B 2-24
Interv.

Anal.
Fr.
Sp.

Zu 5 Noten mit Veränderungen des Bogenstriches.	To be practised 5 notes at a time with variations of the bowing styles.	Sur 5 notes avec changement de coups d'archet.	Sobre 5 notas con cambio de golpes de arco.
Po 5 notách se změnami smyků.	Po 5 nut różnymi smyczkami.	A 5 suoni con cambiamento del colpo d'arco.	Перемены штриховки в группе из 5 нот.

Zu 7 Noten mit Stricharten.
7 notes at a time with bowing styles.
Sur 7 notes avec différents coups d'archet.
Sobre 7 notas con diferentes golpes de arco.
Po 7 notách se smyky.
Po 7 nut różnymi smyczkami.
A 7 note con colpi d'arco.
Группы из 7 нот с различной штриховкой.
a) détaché mf
segue sautillé
b) sautillé mp
zu 9 Noten. – 9 notes at a time. – Sur 9 notes. – Sobre 9 notas.
Po 9 notách. – Po 9 nut. – A 9 note. – Из 9 нот.
a) détaché mf
b) sautillé mp
segue sautillé

B 17-24
Zu 5 Noten mit Stricharten.
Po 5 notách se smyky.
5 notes at a time with bowing styles.
Po 5 nut odmiennymi smyczkami.
Sur 5 notes avec différents coups d'archet.
A 5 note con colpi d'arco.
Sobre 5 notas con diferentes golpes de arco.
По 5 нот различной штриховкой.
a) detaché
b) sautillé
segue sautillé

Zu 7 Noten mit Stricharten.
7 notes at a time with bowing styles.
Sur 7 notes avec différents coups d'archet.
Sobre 7 notas con diferentes golpes de arco.
Po 7 notách se smyky.
Po 7 nut różnymi smyczkami.
A 7 note con colpi d'arco.
По 7 нот различной штриховкой.
a) détaché mf
segue sautillé
b) sautillé mp

Zu 9 Noten mit Stricharten. | 9 notes at a time with bowing styles. | Sur 9 notes avec différents coups d'archet. | Sobre 9 notas con diferentes golpes de arco.

Po 9 notách se smyky. | Po 9 nut różnymi smyczkami. | A 9 note con colpi d'arco. | По 9 нот различной штриховкой.

*) Zuerst ohne Flageolett, um den betreffenden Platz zu finden. Beim Gleiten stark aufdrücken.
**) Mit Flageolett.

*) At first without harmonic, to find the position required. While gliding press hard with finger.
**) With harmonic.

*) Pour trouver la place exacte, travailler d'abord sans l'harmonique. En glissant, appuyer fortement le doigt.
**) Avec son harmonique.

*) Para encontrar el sitio exacto, trabajar primero sin enharmónico. Al deslizar el dedo, apoyarlo con fuerza.
**) Con enharmónico.

*) Napřed bez flageoletu, aby bylo nalezeno jeho příslušné místo. V posouvání silně přitlačiti.
**) S flageoletem.

*) Najpierw bez flageolettu aby osiągnąć pewność danego tonu. Przy posunięciu palec silnie przycisnać.
**) Z flageolettem.

*) Dapprima senza l'armonico per trovare il posto esatto. Durante il portamento premere fortemente.
**) Con armonico.

*) Сперва без flageoletto, чтобы найти нужиое место; при скольжении сильный нажим.
**) C Flageoletto.

C 15-16

C 17-21

*) 3. Lage behalten.

**) In der 2. Lage bleiben.

***) Ohne Flageolett.

*) 3rd position to be held.

**) Remain in third position.

***) Without harmonic.

*) La main reste à la 3ème position.

**) Rester à la 2ème position.

***) Sans son harmonique.

*) La mano se queda en la 3a posición.

**) Quedarse en la 2a posición.

***) Sin enharmónico.

*) Zůstati v 3. poloze.

**) Zůstati v 2. poloze.

***) Bez flageoletu.

*) Pozostać w 3 pozycji.

**) Pozostać w 2 pozycji.

***) Bez flageolettu.

*) Restare alla 3a posizione.

**) Restare alla 2a posizione.

***) Senza armonico.

*) III позицию сохранить.

**) Остаться во II позиции.

***) Без flageoletto

C 31-41

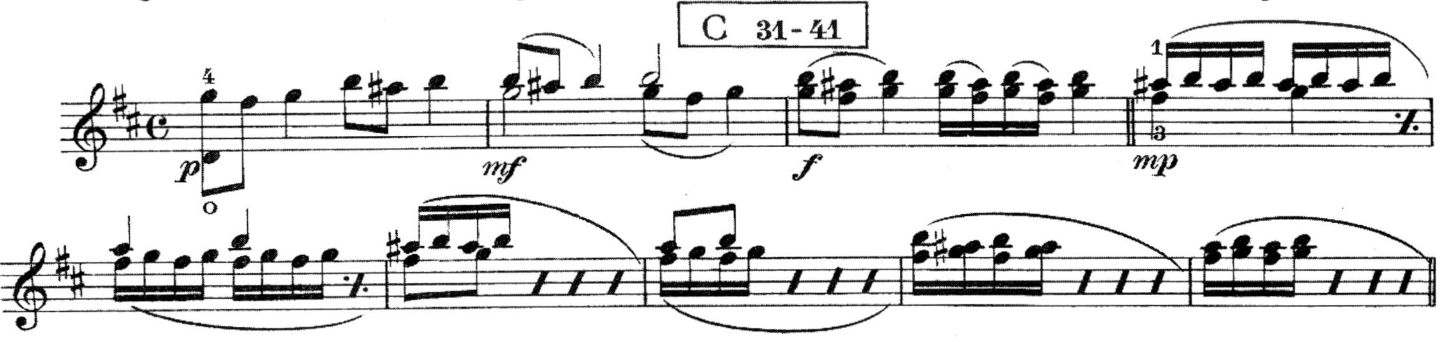

mp
mf
p
cresc.
f
dim.
Fr.
Sp.
C 42-48
tremolo

C 49-65
Interv.
Anal.
Fr.
Sp.

C 63-64

D 30 - E 5
Anal.
E 24 - 32
Interv.
sautillé
Anal.

Die 4 Staccato-Stelle C 49-55, E Takt 25-32 im Zusammenhang.

The 4 staccato-passages C bar 49-55, E bar 25-32 in connection.

Les 4 staccato-placer lettre C mesure 49-55, E mesure 25-32 dans leur rapport.

Los cuatro-staccato-colocar letra C compas 49-55, E compas 25-32 en su relación.

4 staccatová místa C takt 49-55, E takt 25-32 v souvislosti.

4 staccata C takt 49-55, E takt 25-32 w połączeniu.

Le 4 picchiettato lettera C misure 49-55, E misure 25-32 in relazione.

4 staccato C 49-55, E 25 32 в их взаимной связи.

F 20 - 45

Interv.

Anal.
simile
F 24 – 28
Fr.

*) 1. und 4. Finger gleichzeitig vorschieben.

*) 1. a 4. prst současně posouvati.

*) First and fourth fingers advance simultaneously.

*) 1. i 4. palec równocześnie posówać.

*) Avancer en même temps le 1er et le 4ème doigt.

*) Il 1º il 4º dito avanzano nello stesso tempo.

*) Adelantar al mismo tiempo el 1º y 4º dedo.

*) I и IV пальцы продвигать одновременно.

*) Anderer Fingersatz. Schlusspassage.

*) Jiný prstoklad. Závěrečná pasáž.

*) Different fingering. Ending passage.

*) Odmienne opalcowanie. Pasaż końcowy.

*) D'autre doigté. Passage final.

*) Altra diteggiatura. Passaggio finale.

*) Otros doigtés. Pasaje final.

*) Другая разстановка пальцев заключимельный пассаж.

F 41 - 45

Fr. Sp. M. M. M. 8 M. *sautillé* *f* *mf*

Passage F 41 - 45

mit 13 Stricharten. | with 13 bowing variations. | avec 13 variations de coup d'archet. | con 13 variantes de golpes de arco.

s 13 změnami smyku. | 13 różnemi ćwiczeniami smyczkowemi. | con 13 combiamenti di colpi d'arco. | с 13 разными штрихов-ками.

mp *mf* 8 *f*

1 2 M. 3 Fr. 4 M. 5 6 7

8 9 10 Sp. Fr. 11 (Viotti.) 12 M. *spiccato* 13 M. *sautillé*

F 45 - 55

f

ZKRATKY A ZNAČKY.	ABKÜRZUNGEN UND ZEICHEN.		ABBREVIATIONS AND SIGNS.	ABBREVIAZIONI E SEGNI.
Označení délky smyčce zlomky:	Bezeichnung der Bogenlänge durch Bruchzahlen:		Designation of the Length of the Bow by means of fractions:	Indicazione della lunghezza dell'arco per mezzo di frazioni:
Celým smyčcem, půlkou smyčce	Ganzer, halber Bogen	$\frac{1}{1}$ $\frac{1}{2}$	Whole, half Bow	Tutto l'arco, mezzo arco
První, druhou polovinou	Erste, zweite Hälfte	$\frac{1.}{2}$ $\frac{2.}{2}$	First, second Half	Prima metá, seconda metá
Jednou, dvěma třetinami smyčce	Ein, zwei Drittel des Bogens	$\frac{1}{3}$ $\frac{2}{3}$	One, two Third	Un terzo, due terzi, dell'arco
První, druhou, třetí třetinou smyčce	Erstes, zweites, drittes Drittel	$\frac{1.}{3}$ $\frac{2.}{3}$ $\frac{3.}{3}$	First, second, third Third	Primo terzo, secondo terzo, ultimo terzo
Čtvrtinou, třemi čtvrtinami	Ein, drei Viertel	$\frac{1}{4}$ $\frac{3}{4}$	One, three Quarters	Un quarto, tre quarti dell'arco
První, druhou, třetí, čtvrtou čtvrtinou smyčce	Erstes, zweites, drittes, viertes Viertel des Bogens	$\frac{1.}{4}$ $\frac{2.}{4}$ $\frac{3.}{4}$ $\frac{4.}{4}$	First, second, third, fourth Quarter	Primo, secondo, terzo, ultimo quarto dell'arco
Druhou a třetí čtvrtinou smyčce	Zweites und drittes Viertel des Bogens	$\frac{2.\ 3.}{4}$	Second and third Quarters	Secondo e terzo quarto
Dolů	Herunterstrich	⊓	Down-bow	Arco in giu
Nahoru [1])	Hinaufstrich [1])	V	Up-bow [1])	Arco in su [1])
Širokým smykem	Breit gestoßen (gezogen)	—	Broad-bow	Largo staccato
Odráženě (staccato)	Abgestoßen, gehämmert (martellé, staccato)	· ·	Short, detached (staccato)	Staccato, martellato
Skákavě (sautillé; spiccato)	Springend, geworfen (sautillé, spiccato)	▾ ▾	Springing, bounding (sautillé; spiccato; saltato)	Sciolto, sciolto balzato o satellato
Zvednouti smyčec	Bogen heben	’	Lift Bow	Alzare l'arco
Zvednouti druhý prst	Zweiten Finger heben	(2	Lift the 2nd. Finger	Alzare il dito secondo
Odsadit (umělá pomlka) [2])	Kunstpause (Luftpause) [2])	|	Stop (artificial pause) [2])	Pausa artistica (respiro musicale) [2])
I První struna E, II druhá struna A, III třetí struna D, IV čtvrtá struna G.	I erste Saite E, II zweite Saite A, III dritte Saite D, IV vierte Saite G.	I II III IV	I first String E, II second String A, III third String D, IV fourth String G	I corda di *mi*, II corda di *la*, III corda di *re*, IV corda di *sol*
Prázdná struna	Leere Saite	o	Open String	Corda vuota
Levá ruka od hmatníku, při čemž se smyčec ponechá na struně	Die linke Hand weg vom Griffbrett bei Belassung des Bogens auf der Saite	♪	The left hand off the finger board, the bow remaining on the string	Levare la mano sinistra dalla tastiera, lasciando l'arco sulla corda
Na struně E	Auf der E-Saite	sul E	On the E-string	Sulla corda di *mi*
První prst zůstane na struně	Liegenlassen des 1. Fingers	1____	First Finger remains on string	Lasciare il primo dito sulla Corda
Prst, na nějž ukazuje háček, zůstane ležet	Liegenlassen des Fingers, auf welchen das Häkchen zeigt	└____	The little hook indicates which Finger is to remain on string	Questo segno indica quale dito deve restare sulla corda
Trylek	Triller	*tr*	Trills	Trillo
Vibrato, tremolo	Vibrato, Tremolo	〰	Vibrato, Tremolo	Vibrato, tremolo
Pizzicato: brnká se pravou rukou	Pizzicato mit der rechten Hand	pizz.	Pizzicato with the right hand	Pizzicato colla mano destra
Pizzicato: brnká se levou rukou	Pizzicato (kneifen) mit der linken Hand	+	Pizzicato with the left hand	Pizzicato colla mano sinistra
Glissando — sklouznout	Glissando, gleiten	*gliss.*	Glissando — gliding	Glissando
Středem smyčce	Mitte des Bogens	M.	Middle of the Bow	Alla metá dell'arco
U žabky smyčce	Am Frosch	Fr.	At the Nut	Tallone
Hrotem smyčce	An der Spitze	Sp.	At the Point	Punta dell'arco
(hranatá nota s nožkou) Flageolet	(Quadrat mit Fuß) Flageoletton	◇ (with stem)	(footed Square) Harmonic tone	(Quadrato col gambo) Flautato (armonico)
(hranatá nota bez nožky) Opěrný prst	(Quadrat ohne Fuß) Stummer Stützfinger oder Lagenverbindungston	◇	(without Foot) Passive suporting Finger or Transitiontone	(Quadrato senza gambo) Dito d'appogio muto oppure suono legante le posizioni
Cvičení k 2.-4. taktu ze sóla	Übung zum 2-4 Takt aus dem Solo	[2-4]	Study for 2.-4. bar from the Solo	Studio per 2-4 battuta di Solo

[1]) *bez označení smyku začíná počáteční takt vždy od žabky.*

[2]) *Zvednouti smyčec a učiniti krátkou pomlku.*

[1]) *Ohne Bezeichnung der Richtung, beginnt der Anfangstakt immer am Frosch.*

[2]) *Bogen heben und kurze Pause machen.*

[1]) *Unless otherwise indicated, the first measure begins at the nut.*

[2]) *Lift Bow and make a brief pause.*

[1]) *Senza l'indicazione della direzione cominciare sempre al tallone.*

[2]) *Alzare l'arco facendo una breve pausa.*

Piano Score

CONCERTO No. 2

for Violin and Orchestra

I.

H. Wieniawski, Op. 22.

pizz.
p
Vla.
Cl.
Fg.
1.2.Cor.
p
A
Meno mosso.
p
Fg.
Vc.
mf
Fg.
CB.
Vl.1.
Vla.
Vc.
Vc.
Animato.
Vla
Fg.
Vc.
mf
pizz.
Cl.
Vl.1
Fg.
Vl.2.
Vla
Fl.
Ob.
Cl.
f
Tutti
ff

Holz(legni)
Quint
2. Ob.
Quart.
ff
p
Fg.
CB.
Trb.
f
Tempo più tranquillo
-de
morendo
Quint.
ff
p
Timp.
B
dolce ma sotto voce
Vl.1.2.
mf
Vla
p
Timp.
Vc.
p
mf
1.Fl.
p
Quint.
rall.
rall.

a tempo
cresc.
a tempo
Holz. [legni]
accel.
rall. al tempo
Quint.
Vl. 1. 2.
Vla.
Bassi
C
Meno mosso.
Vl. 1.
Bassi
m. d.
tranquillo
Vc.
dolce
rit.
a tempo
Quint.
appass

cresc.
Holz.
f con fuoco
f
cresc.
f
Quart.
f
D
(♩= 108)
rit.
p
cresc.
p
Vl.1.2.
Vla.
rit.
p
Bassi
f
mf
dim.
p
cresc.
1. 2. Cl.
p
1. 2. Fg.
Vl.1.
f
mf
dim.
p
cresc.
Vl.2
p
1. 2. Cl.
p
1. 2. Fg.
Vla
p
Vc.
p
dim.
f
Vl.1.
p
p
Quart.
Vla
p

1. Cl. Solo
p
pizz.
Cl.
Fl.
Cl.
f
Vl. 1. 2.
pizz
pp
cresc.
Fg. Vla
sf
Bassi
f
E
<appassionato>
Vl. 1. 2.
Vla
p
Bassi
f
1. Fl.
f
Vl. 1.
mf
f
1. Fg
Vl. 1.

fp
ff
cresc.
con fuoco
poco a
f
ff Holz.
poco tranquillo
rall.
(♩= 92)
p semplice
Ob.
p
Quart.
rall.
1. Cor.
pp
pp Vc.
p
mf
pp
Vl. 1.
f
Bassi
F
sf
Fl.
Cl.
Fg.
p
Vc.
Ob.
p
Quint.
espressivo
Vc.

mf
Vl.1.
Vla.
p
rit.
pp
1. Fl.
rit.
f energico
mf
p
mp
f
f
p
Bassi
Ob.
sf
sf
fz
Vl.1.
più animato
f
più animato
p
p
pizz.
sf
sf
sf
sf
sf
f
fz
Vl.1.
1.2. Cor.

largamente
Cl.Fg.
G
pizz.
Vl.1.
1.2. Cor.
Vc.
Holz
rall.
(♩ = 116)
Quint.
rall.
Vc.
pizz.

Vc.
ff
Fl.
Bassi
2 Cl.
1. Corno
H
restez
Vl.1.
Vla.
Vc.
cresc.
ffp
Fl.
Ob.
Cl.
Hbl.
(Legni)
Cor.
mf

fz
mf
Quint.
p
f
ff
Tutti
ff
Fg.
Cor.
Vc.
CB.
Vl.1.
Vla.
Vc.
Holz (Legni)
Vl.1.
Fg.
Cor.
Vc.
CB.
I
Vc.
f
m.g.
m.d.
Fl.
Vl.1.
Fg.
Cor
Vl.1.
p tranqu.
cresc.

Vl.1.
Vla.
Fl.
Cl.
Vl.
Vc.
p
Bassi
pizz.
f
Ped.
Holz
Cor.
ff
Quint.
p
Fg.1.
Cor.
Cl.
Fg.2.
Cl.1.
L'istesso tempo.
pizz.
Vc.
1. Cl. Solo

II.
Romance.

A
Cl
Vl.1.
Cl.
poco rit.
a tempo
Vla.
Vc.
espress.
rall.
Ob.

agitato (♩. = 72)
f molto sonore
Vla
Fg.
Bassi
ff
mf
Fl.
p
Ob.
Vl.1. pizz.
sf
Fl.
Vl.1.
Cl.
B
p
mp
Cl.
Vl.1.
Fg.
p
p Vc.
mf
1.Cor.
animato (♩. = 80)
p
mf
Ob
p animato
cresc.
f
più mosso
Vl.1.
più mosso
cresc.
Ob.
f

rall.
sf
mf
p
Vl. 1
Bassi
Vc.
Tempo I.
p dolce
pp
ff
pp dolcissimo
f
cresc.
ffz
dim.

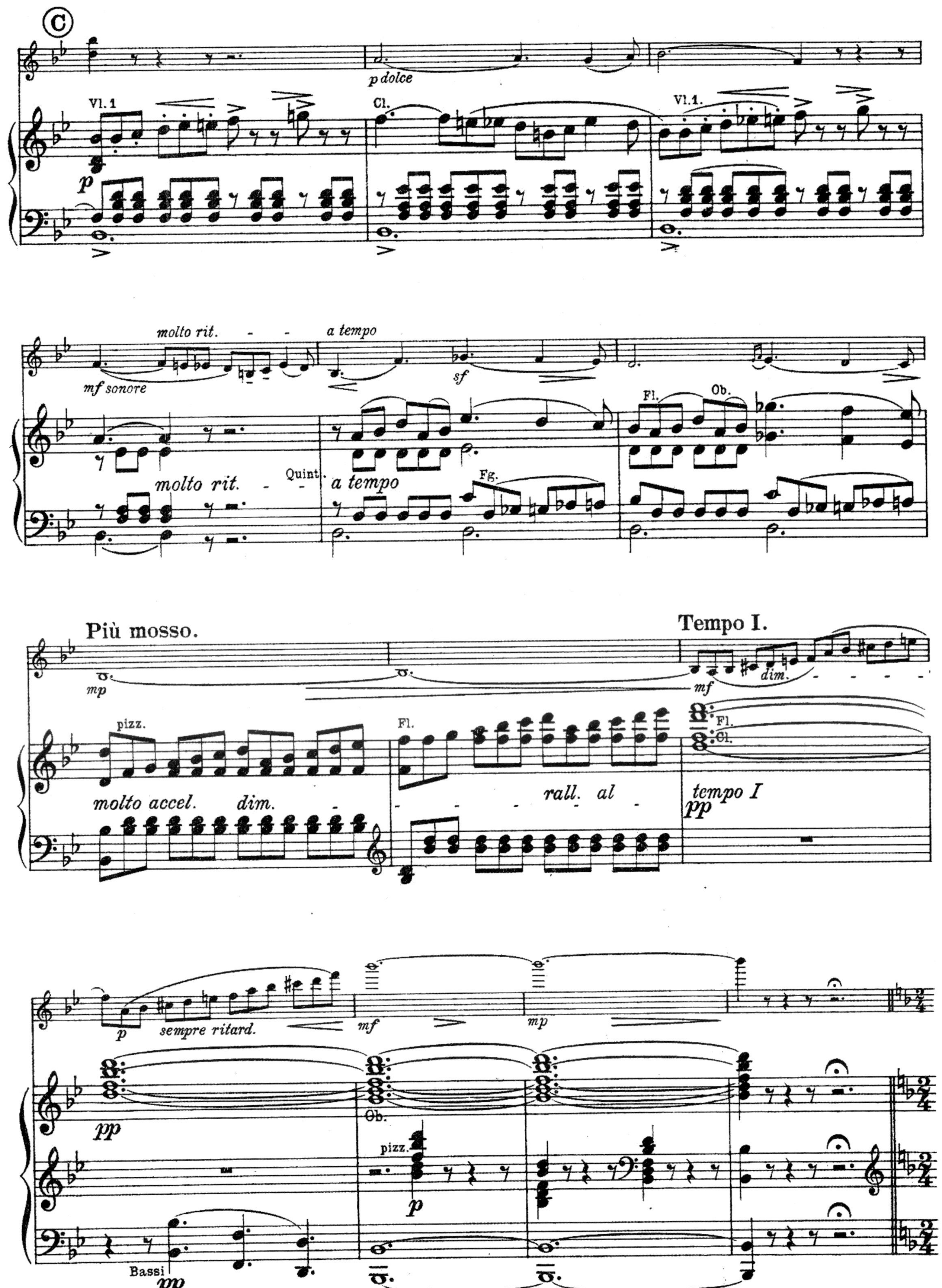
C
p dolce
Vl. 1
Cl.
Vl. 1.
p
molto rit.
a tempo
mf sonore
sf
Fl.
Ob.
molto rit.
Quint.
a tempo
Fg.
Più mosso.
Tempo I.
mp
mf
dim.
pizz.
Fl.
Fl.
Cl.
molto accel.
dim.
rall. al
tempo I
pp
p
sempre ritard.
mf
mp
pp
Ob.
pizz.
p
Bassi
pp

D Allegro con fuoco. (♩= 120)
f
Vl.
f
Vla.
f
f
mp
sfz
Vl.
cre - - scen - - do
f
f
fp leggiero
Cadenza
fp
mf
f
Lento.
Vivo.
ff
rit. e dim.
pp
ppp

III.

A la Zingara.

Vla. pizz.
Vl.
Vc.
Holz
Bassi
cre - scen - do
Quart.
Tempo poco rit.
Tutti

poco a poco rit.

poco a

poco rit.

Fl.

Ob.

Vc.pizz.

poco più tranquillo (♩ = 92)

poco più tranquillo

Fl.

Cl.

Vla.

Bassi

cresc.

Cl.2

agitato

Ob.

agitato

appassionato e cresc.

Vl.1.

Vl.2

ff molto appassionato

Cl.

Vc.

alargare
molto vibrato
rit.
Cl.
Fg.
p rit.
Bassi
B
(♩ = 116)
simile
f saltando
Quart.
fp
simile
sautillé
détaché
sautillé
fp
1. Cor.
p
Timp.
pp

8
f détaché
Fl.
Ob.
p
mf
C
Lento.
Vivo.
poco rit. e dim.
poco rit.
Quint.
Timp.
p
a tempo (♩ = 108)
f
f
a tempo
fp
Vc. pizz.
Holz
p
Corni
Quint.
f
sf
f
pizz.
allongez
Fl. Cl.
p
f
f
3
p
Timp.
Vc. pizz.
3
3
p alargando
Vl. 1. 2.
p
Vla

risoluto
f
sf
Vl.1
arco
Vla
C.B.
Bassi pizz.
rit.
ff
accel.
Quint.
fp
Corni
Fg.
Quart.
sf
p
Vla
D
a tempo risoluto, ma moderato
Vc. Fg.
ff

poco rit.
mf
mp
Fl.
Cl.
Ob.
mp
poco rit.
Cor.
Vc. pizz.
dolce e più tranquillo
Cl.
Vla
Vl. 1
dolce e più tranquillo
p
Cl.
Cl.
p
Ob.
p
Vl. 1
p
appassionato
Fg.
appass.
Vla
ff

molto appassionato
alargare
Fl.
Ob.
Tempo I.
E
sf
f
Quart.
p
1. Fl.
p
accelerando
Vla pizz.
Vc.
simile
Fg.
8
Vl.1
mf
f
p
Vl.1.2. Vla pizz.

Ob.
Ob.
Fl.
Vla pizz.
Vl.
Vc.
Holz
F
Fg.1.2.
Cor.1
Vc. pizz.
Holz
Corni
Quint.
allongez
pizz.
Fl.Cl.
Tr.
Timp.
Vc. pizz.

sf
Holz
pizz.
Tr.
fz
f Quint. arco
f
8
fz
ff brillante con fuoco
Vl. 1.2
f
Vl. Vla
Holz
mp
mf
p
f
Tutti
(senza Tromb.)
ff
Tutti

OTAKAR ŠEVČÍK Op. 17

Wieniawski Violin Concerto in D minor

Critical Urtext Violin Part

Edited by Endre Granat

Violin solo

CONCERTO No. 2

for Violin and Orchestra

Edited by Endre Granat

HENRYK WIENIAWSKI
Op. 22

dolce
(Poco più vivo)
D
(p molto legato)
(f)

cresc.

E

appassionato

(*mp* *cresc.*)

(*f*)

poco rit.

(Tempo I)

p semplice

F

Più animato
G

III
H
II
restez
restez
(cresc.)
de la pointe
rit.
I
L'istesso tempo

ROMANCE
Andante non troppo
p
III
A
III
IV
III
poco rit.
(a tempo)
p
III
espressivo
a tempo
IV
Animato
III
B
p

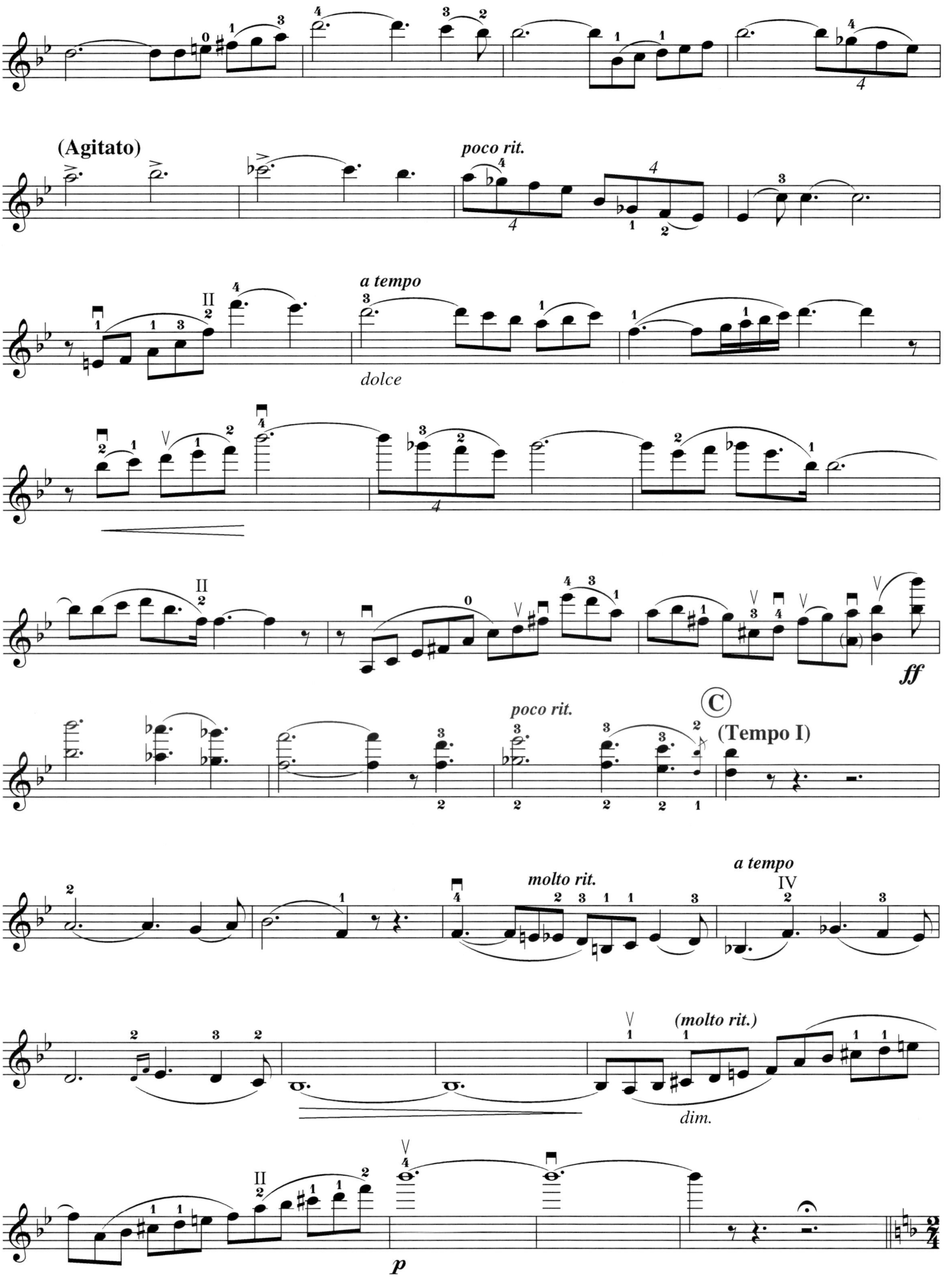

(Agitato)

poco rit.

a tempo

dolce

ff

Ⓒ

poco rit.

(Tempo I)

molto rit.

a tempo

(molto rit.)

dim.

p

D
Allegro con fuoco
(f)
(f)
(cresc.)
(ff)
Cadenza
(f)
(fp) leggiero
(cresc.)
(f)
IV
rit.
dim.

A
Allegro moderato (à la Zingara)
p
8va
p tranquillo
Tutti
f

poco a poco rit.
poco più tranquillo
appassionato
cresc.
molto appassionato
(poco rit.)
du talon
molto vibrato
B
saltando

C
poco rit.
dim.
(a tempo)
IV
f
II
p a piacere
(cresc.)
(f)
f p
D
8va
5

poco rit.
più tranquillo
dolce
(con passione)
appassionato
E
rit.
Tempo I (Allegro moderato)

(allargando)
F
(a tempo)
f
IV
8va
ff brillante con fuoco
stringendo
ff

SELECTED VIOLIN SOLO AND CHAMBER MUSIC

Violin

Violin Etudes and Instruction

Wohlfahrt, Franz

S510005 Sixty Etudes for Violin, Op. 45, Bk. 1 HL 42303

2011 new issues--former Strad Magazine Editor-in-Chief, Eric Wen re-examines these classics with consideration for today's violinist. All editions newly engraved with handsome color covers and classic 9x12 ivory stock.

ed. Eric Wen

S510006 Sixty Etudes for Violin, Op. 45, Bk. 2 HL 42391

Violin Solo, unaccompanied

Adolphe, Bruce

X510011 Bitter, Sour, Salt Suite HL 41866

Can be performed with or without narration, soloist can narrate.

Baker, David

S510001 Suite for Unaccompanied Violin HL 40248

Recorded by Ruggerio Ricci on Laurel Records

Hartke, Stephen

X510012 Caoine HL 41867

Name derived from the laments once sung by the professional wailing women of Ireland; also inspired by the folk fiddling tradition of the Shetland Islands.

Perkinson, Coleridge-Taylor

X510033 Blue/s Forms HL 41886

Three-movement solo violin work fusing blues harmonic language with classical sonata form, recorded by Sanford Allen.

X510032 Louisiana Blues Strut: A Cakewalk HL 41885

Recorded by Sanford Allen on Cedille Records "Coleridge-Taylor Perkinson: A Celebration"

Violin Solo with Keyboard

Baker, David

X511007 Blues (Deliver My Soul) HL 41894

Recorded by Anne Akiko Meyers and Andre Michel-Schub, BMG Records..

S511005 Ethnic Variations on a Theme of Paganini HL 40254

Commissioned By Ruggerio Ricci.

Cooman, Carson

X511035 Sonata for Violin and Organ HL 41918

Crockett, Donald

X511039 Wet Ink for Violin and Piano HL 42418

Violin and piano version of nonet by the same title, dedicated to Steven Stucky for his 60th birthday.

Dancla, Charles

S511010 Six Airs Varies for Violin and Piano, Op. 89 HL 42368

2011 new issues--former Strad Magazine Editor-in-Chief, Eric Wen re-examines these classics with consideration for today's violinist. All editions newly engraved with handsome color covers and classic 9x12 ivory stock.

ed. Eric Wen

Sevcik, Otakar

S511012 Sevcik Op. 16 Wieniawski Scherzo-Tarantelle with Analytical Exercises HL 42327

Combines urtext quality solo material with exercises based on renowned 20th-Century violin pedagogue, Otakar Sevcik's, work.

ed. Stephen Shipps

S511014 Sevcik Op. 17 Wieniawski Concerto Op. 22 in D Minor with Analytical Exercises HL TBDS511014

ed. Endre Granat

S511013 Sevcik Op. 19 Tchaikovsky Concerto Op. 35 in D Major with Analytical Exercises HL TBDS511013

ed. Stephen Shipps

S511011 Sevcik Op. 21 Mendelssohn Violin Concerto in e minor with Analytical Exercises HL 42326

ed. Endre Granat

Smith, John Stafford

S511015 The Star-Spangled Banner (Arranged for Violin and Piano by Jascha Heifetz) HL 42616

Along with new engraving for his celebrated transcription, a photo from master violinist Jascha Heifetz's historical collection and a facsimile of the original autograph score adorn this commemorative 9x12 edition.

Stock, David

X511020 Santa Fe Salsa HL 41905

For Andres Cardenes

Walker, George

X511038 Concerto for Violin and Orchestra (Piano reduction) HL 42310

Dedicated to Violinist and Composer Gregory T.S. Walker. Recorded by Gregory Walker, violin and Sinfonia Varsovia, Ian Hobson Conductor, on Albany Records.

Walker, Gwyneth

X511015 Fantasy Etudes HL 41900

Suite of short pieces which can be enjoyed by performers of all ages.

Violin Duo

Hartke, Stephen

X512001 Oh Them Rats Is Mean in My Kitchen HL 41921

Scherzo-fantasy in homage to early blues, transforming its characteristic wailing and energetic speech-song into the seemingly incongruous medium of the violin duo

X512003 Two Shetland Bridal Tunes HL 41923

Two arrangements of traditional Shetland Island fiddle tunes encompassing a processional and recessional, for any festive event or occasion.

Trios, mixed

Violin

Hartke, Stephen

X632711 The Horse with the Lavender Eye for Violin, Clarinet and Piano HL 42074

Four movement tableau of vivid musical images bound together with skillfully crafted 'off-balance' motifs